52

UNCOMMON DATES

A COUPLE'S ADVENTURE GUIDE
FOR PRAYING, PLAYING,
AND STAYING TOGETHER

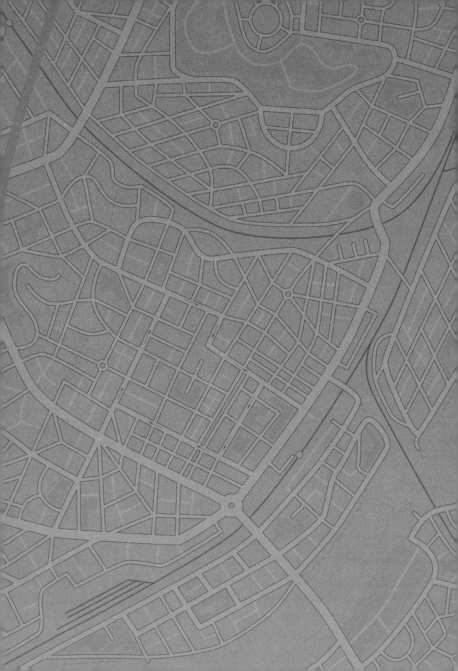

52 UNCOMMON DATES

A COUPLE'S ADVENTURE GUIDE FOR PRAYING, PLAYING, AND STAYING TOGETHER

RANDY SOUTHERN

MOODY PUBLISHERS

CHICAGO

Manuscript created with the assistance of Christopher Hudson & Associates, Inc. (www.HudsonBible.com).

All Scripture quotations, unless otherwise indicated, are taken from the *Holy Bible, New Living Translation*, copyright © 1996, 2004. Used by permission of Tyndale House Publishers, Inc., Wheaton, Illinois 60189, U.S.A. All rights reserved.

Interior and cover design: Julia Ryan / www.DesignByJulia
Cover images: Twig art of "5" © Shutterstock/Ron & Joe; background generic city map © Shutterstock/Robert Adrian Hillman; "2" © Shutterstock/Roman Siggev; illustration © Julia Ryan; paper strips © Graphicstock.com.

Library of Congress Cataloging-in-Publication Data

52 uncommon dates : a couple's adventure guide for praying, playing, and staying together.
     pages cm
   Summary: "52 Uncommon Dates ignites a prayerful and playful connection in a way that feels natural for couples to schedule and relate to real life. Fun, creative, and spiritually engaging, this powerful resource will revive the relational, physical, emotional and spiritual aspects of your relationship, one date at a time"-- Provided by publisher.
   ISBN 978-0-8024-1174-7 (paperback)
   1. Dating (Social customs) 2. Dating (Social customs)--Religious aspects--Christianity.
   3. Marriage--Religious aspects--Christianity. 4. Interpersonal relations--Religious aspects--Christianity. I. Title. II. Title: Fifty-two uncommon dates.
   HQ801.S6762 2014
   241'.676--dc23

                              2014006898

We hope you enjoy this book from Moody Publishers. Our goal is to provide high-quality, thought-provoking books and products that connect truth to your real needs and challenges. For more information on other books and products written and produced from a biblical perspective, go to *www.moodypublishers.com* or write to:

Moody Publishers
820 N. La Salle Boulevard
Chicago, IL 60610

CONTENTS

INTRODUCTION

Many couples stop dating when they get married. Their minds say, "Okay, we're through with the dating stage. We've reached our goal. We are now married. So let's get on with the more important stuff of life such as work, completing an education, acquiring a house, and perhaps having a baby." Dating is viewed as a prelude to marriage. It was important, it served its purpose, but now it's time to get serious about life.

It is this kind of reasoning that leads couples to forget that their relationship with each other is what marriage is all about. The vocations, cars, houses, and other possessions will become meaningless if the relationship dies. Thousands of divorced individuals have walked this road. Marriages must be nurtured if they are to flourish. They are not nurtured when all of our time and energy are spent on other pursuits, even the raising of children. The best thing we can do for our children is to keep our marriages vibrant and growing.

Dating is to marriage what breathing is to the body. It brings in fresh oxygen to nourish the cells of matrimony. Couples who continue dating after the wedding are far more likely to have a healthy marriage. The choice to date communicates the message, "I still love you. I still enjoy being with you. I'm still glad I married you." However, in order to make dating a reality we face several challenges.

First is the challenge of time. There are so many voices calling for our attention; the loudest of which is our vocation and/or graduate studies. Both of these pursuits require large chunks of our time. Beyond that is what we commonly call household chores: cooking, washing dishes, vacuuming floors, doing the laundry, cleaning toilets, and so forth. And, of course, there is the call of sleep, which, if it is not heeded, will influence all the rest of life.

One wife said, "I would love for us to date, but I simply don't have time." So what is the answer to the time dilemma? I believe it is found in one word: *prioritize*! We decide the things that are important in our lives. Once we rank them as highly important, we make time for them. Most of us make time to eat and sleep because we value these as extremely important to life. If we see our marriage relationship as being high priority, we can make time for dating.

The second challenge is creating a positive, emotional climate so we enjoy being together. This is why it is so important that we discover and learn to speak each other's primary love language. The euphoria of the "in love" experience has evaporated. We must consciously choose to speak love to our spouse in a language that touches their emotions. My book *The 5 Love Languages* has helped millions of couples learn how to keep emotional love alive through the years. The second essential in creating a positive emotional climate is dealing effectively with our failures. None of us are perfect. We sometimes say and do things that hurt each other. These hurts do not simply go away with the passing of time. We must be willing to apologize for our failures and willing to forgive each other. Without apologies and forgiveness, we will build an emotional barrier between us. Such barriers discourage dating.

When we learn to communicate love effectively and deal realistically with our failures, we create a positive, emotional climate that encourages us to enjoy life together. This kind of climate encourages us to continue dating after marriage.

The third challenge is what to do on a date. We are creatures of habit, and we tend to get into ruts. Going to the same restaurants and doing the same thing date after date eventually becomes mundane. We are hardly aware we are dating; we are now simply going out to eat. This is where Randy Southern offers help in *52 Uncommon Dates.* The word *uncommon* means unusual. I can assure you that many of the dates Randy suggests are unusual. They are not things you would likely come up with on your own, but once you try them, you will be glad you did. If you date once a week, this book provides a full year of suggestions. If you date every other week, here are two years of suggestions. If you get out only once a month, you can look forward to more than four years of uncommon dates you will never forget.

52 Uncommon Dates will help you plan and execute meaningful dates with your spouse, which in turn will give you a vibrant, growing marriage, which is, in fact, the marriage you've always wanted.

GARY CHAPMAN, PHD

WHAT ARE THE FIVE LOVE LANGUAGES?
WHAT IS YOURS?

WORDS OF AFFIRMATION

Actions don't always speak louder than words. If this is your love language, unsolicited compliments mean the world to you. Hearing the words "I love you" is important—hearing the reasons behind that love sends your spirits skyward.

QUALITY TIME

Nothing says "I love you" like full, undivided attention. Being there for a person whose love language is Quality Time is critical, but really being there—with the TV off, fork and knife down, and all chores and tasks on standby—makes him or her feel truly special and loved.

RECEIVING GIFTS

The receiver of gifts thrives on the love, thoughtfulness, and effort behind the gift. If you speak this language, the perfect gift or gesture shows that you are known, you are cared for, and you are prized above whatever was sacrificed to bring the gift to you.

ACTS OF SERVICE

Anything you do to ease the burden of responsibilities weighing on an Acts of Service person will speak volumes. The words he or she most wants to hear: "Let me do that for you."

PHYSICAL TOUCH

A person whose primary language is Physical Touch enjoys hugs, pats on the back, and thoughtful touches on the arm. These can all be ways to show excitement, concern, care, and love.

Visit 5lovelanguages.com to discover your primary love language!

THE FIRST TIME FOR EVERYTHING DATE

WORDS TO GROW ON

For God has not given us a spirit of fear and timidity, but of power, love, and self-discipline.

2 TIMOTHY 1:7

You don't have to have money to keep romance alive in a marriage. But you do have to be thoughtful.

GARY CHAPMAN

SET THE SCENE

God created us with a capacity to enjoy a wide variety of experiences. Too often, though, we limit ourselves by "sticking to what we know." We hang out in the places where we feel most comfortable— with the people who make us feel comfortable. We talk about the things we know. We wear a groove in our comfort zone that over time becomes a rut.

If that sounds familiar to you, then this is where you reverse the trend and pull out of that rut. On this date, nothing will feel familiar or comfortable because everything you do will be a first for you.

MAKE IT HAPPEN

The best way to approach this date is to consider your natural instincts—and then do the opposite. Here are some things you'll need to think about.

1 *Change your venue.*
Find a nearby town or an area of the city that neither of you has ever stepped foot in. Start your date there.

2 *Expand your palate.*
What's the most eclectic (yet affordable) restaurant in the area? What's the strangest thing on its menu? Start your ordering there. From appetizers to desserts, the only rule is this: don't eat anything that's crossed your palate before.

3 *Explore a new form of entertainment.*
Ever been to a jazz club? A Roller Derby match? Open mic night at a comedy club? A high school play? A patch of ground just beyond the airport runway where you can sit and watch planes take off and land?

4 *Keep the conversation fresh.*
If most of your date-night conversations involve your jobs or the kids, this is the night to declare those topics off-limits. Anything you've never discussed before is fair game.

5 *Add a new spice to your lovemaking.*
Married couples can continue the first-time-for-everything theme in your physical intimacy. Is there a room in your house you haven't "initiated"? Is there a sexual position you haven't tried? If you're both comfortable with an idea and have never tried it before, this is the time.

FINISH STRONG

Before you end your First Time for Everything Date, spend a few minutes talking about the experience and what you'll take away from it. Use the following questions as needed to guide your discussion:

- ► What was the best part of the date?

- ► Was your conversation better, or just different, because you avoided your regular conversation topics?

- ► Would you want to do a First Time for Everything Date again sometime, or was this one time enough?

MIND YOUR LANGUAGE

If your date's primary love language is Receiving Gifts, this would be a great date to surprise the person you love the most with something truly unique. It doesn't have to be expensive or even necessarily useful. Just make sure it's something different from any other gift they have ever received.

TAKE IT TO GOD

Before your date, spend some time in prayer together. Thank God for the variety of people and situations He's put in your path. Thank Him for His blessings and mercies, which are *new* every morning. In the spirit of this date theme, ask Him to

- ▶ show you areas of your life in which you're in danger of falling into a rut;
- ▶ give you the creativity and courage to try new things to escape or avoid a rut;
- ▶ help you keep your relationship fresh and exciting;
- ▶ help you maintain an adventurous spirit in your Christian walk.

DIG DEEP

The Christian life is all about newness and freshness. The Bible tells us "that anyone who belongs to Christ has become a new person" (2 Corinthians 5:17). The last thing a new person needs is to get stuck in an old rut. If you want to be inspired to live more adventurously, check out the following passages:

- ▶ Psalm 92:12–14
- ▶ Lamentations 3:22–23
- ▶ Luke 5:36–39
- ▶ Colossians 3:10
- ▶ Devotional reading from *The Love Languages Devotional Bible*, page 334

TO NEXT DATE

THE CEMETERY DATE

WORDS TO GROW ON

*Therefore, since we are surrounded by such a
huge crowd of witnesses to the life of faith,
let us strip off every weight that slows us down,
especially the sin that so easily trips us up.
And let us run with endurance the race
God has set before us.*

HEBREWS 12:1

*On George Washington Carver's tombstone
are carved the following words: "He could
have added fortune to fame, but caring for
neither, he found happiness and honor in
being helpful to the world." People of all races
still honor George Washington Carver.
Why? Because he lived a self-sacrificing life
for the benefit of others.
True honor is always earned.*

GARY CHAPMAN

2

SET THE SCENE

At first glance, this may seem like a morbid, even unsettling, idea for a date. That's why it's important to set the right tone. Reading Hebrews 12:1 together to start your date would be an ideal tone-setter.

Visiting burial sites together can serve as a reminder of those who have run God's course and lived victorious Christian lives before us. Your purpose is to honor them and to remind each other that other people—the living and the dead—can positively influence us in our spiritual success.

MAKE IT HAPPEN

Here are some tips for planning a memorable and meaningful cemetery date.

1 *Choose a place that has a personal connection to you.*
If you have family members buried in a local cemetery, start there. Visit their graves. (If you're so inclined, bring flowers.) Share a few memories. After you've paid your respects, you can widen your circle of exploration.

2 *Look for eye-catching grave markers.*
Which ones really stand out from the rest? What can you conclude about those people based on the way they're memorialized? Do you think they had any input in choosing their gravestones, or do you think their gravestones were chosen by relatives after their deaths?

Talk about the kind of grave marker you would prefer. What would the design be? What would you want it to say? Why?

3 *Let the dates on the gravestones tell you stories.*
If you can do the math to figure out how old people were when they died, you can make educated guesses as to what their lives may have been like. Think about the person who out-lived a spouse by thirty years. Think about the mother who lost a child in infancy. Think about the person who's buried alone.

4 *Talk about your personal crowd of witnesses.*
Think about the Christians in your life who have died. How did their faithfulness to God influence you in your Christian walk? Are you encouraged in your faith by the testimony they left behind? Or does remembering them make you feel guilty when you make a mess of things?

FINISH STRONG

Before you end your Cemetery Date, spend a few minutes talking together about the experience and what you'll take away from it. Use the following questions as needed to guide your discussion:

▶ Was the date eerie or comforting?

▶ Did seeing the gravestones make you want to prioritize anything differently in life? Explain.

▶ What gravestone affected you the most, and why?

MIND YOUR LANGUAGE

If your date's primary love language is Words of Affirmation, share a list of epitaphs that could be used on their gravestone. (Again, do your best to skirt the morbid aspects of the exercise and focus on making your date feel loved, appreciated, and affirmed.)

Here are a few ideas to get your creative juices flowing:

- ▶ She made her husband the luckiest man in the world.
- ▶ He brought color to the world.
- ▶ She changed lives.
- ▶ Everyone who knew him was better for it.

 ## TAKE IT TO GOD

Before your date, spend some time in prayer together. Thank God for the life He gives—in this world and throughout eternity. Thank Him for the people who made a difference in your life before they died. Ask God to

- ▶ help you maintain a proper perspective during your date;
- ▶ remind you when you're feeling discouraged that a crowd of witnesses have run the course before you;
- ▶ give you the endurance and strength to finish the race set before you.

DIG DEEP

Looking for more passages that talk about staying strong in the Christian faith and completing the course that is laid out before you? Try these:

- ▶ Joshua 1:9
- ▶ 1 Chronicles 16:11
- ▶ Isaiah 40:31
- ▶ 1 Corinthians 10:13
- ▶ Philippians 4:13

- ▶ Devotional reading from *The Love Languages Devotional Bible*, page 353

TO NEXT DATE

THE MUSIC DATE

WORDS TO GROW ON

Come, let us sing to the Lord! Let us shout joyfully to the Rock of our salvation.

PSALM 95:1

Music expresses the rhythm and rhyme of [our] hearts.

GARY CHAPMAN

3

SET THE SCENE

Whether you're a hard-core geek with thousands of albums, CDs, and downloads in your collection (ahem) or someone who just enjoys singing along to the radio, you've been affected by music to some degree. Music is one of God's greatest gifts.

Music is the soundtrack of life. It defines eras and marks significant events—both cultural and personal.

It's only natural, then, that music should play a role in your relationship. Do you remember the song that was playing the first time you saw each other? Do you remember the first time your significant other turned up the radio and said, "I love this song"? Are

there certain song lyrics that remind you of the other person and bring a smile to your face every time you hear them? If so, why not spend an evening celebrating your favorite music with your favorite person?

MAKE IT HAPPEN

As is the case with most of the ideas in this book, the more preparation you put into your date, the bigger the payoff will likely be. There are a few different ways you can approach your date.

1 *Create separate playlists in advance and play them for each other during your date.*
The bigger your music library is, the better your playlist will be. If you don't have the tunes you want on your device, raid the collection of a music-geek friend. Ask for input and find out about some songs or artists you may not be aware of.

2 *Take turns playing songs from your music library that mean something to you.*
Scroll through the list and look for songs that tug at your heart, spark a memory, or take you back to certain times or events in your life.

3 *Go to a used record store, find some romantic CDs, take them home, and dance to the songs.*
Talk about money well spent. If you've never slow danced together, this is the time.

FINISH STRONG

Before you end your Music Date, spend a few minutes talking together about the experience and what you'll take away from it. Use the following questions as needed to guide your discussion:

► What song brought the most interesting conversation to the date?

► Did including music in the date affect your emotions at all during the date? How?

► If we didn't have a "song" as a couple, do we now, after this date?

 ## MIND YOUR LANGUAGE

If your date's primary love language is Quality Time (and if this Music Date is a success), try it again in a different venue. Go for a drive together —the longer, the better. If you don't have a destination in mind, go for a nice jaunt in the country, like your grandparents might have done.

Leave your distractions at home. All you'll need is each other and a playlist of favorite songs. Spend a few hours singing and listening together. Talk about your reactions to certain tunes. Reminisce about the first time you heard them. Fill your car with music and your date's love tank with Quality Time.

TAKE IT TO GOD

Before your date, spend some time in prayer together. Thank God for His gift of music and the influence it's had on your lives. While you're at it, why not have a quick worship time by singing your favorite praise song together? Seems appropriate, doesn't it? Ask God to

- ► bless your time with each other;
- ► free your minds from distractions so you can focus completely on your date;
- ► help you shed your inhibitions and self-consciousness so you can fully enjoy God's gift of music together.

DIG DEEP

Throughout its pages, the Bible encourages God's people to enjoy music and use it in our worship. See for yourself in these passages:

- ► Psalm 71:23
- ► Psalm 105:2
- ► Ephesians 5:19
- ► Colossians 3:16

- ► James 5:13
- ► Devotional reading from *The Love Languages Devotional Bible*, page 584

TO NEXT DATE

THE GET LOST DATE

WORDS TO GROW ON

I can never escape from your Spirit!
I can never get away from your presence!

PSALM 139:7

At the end of time, when all history culminates
in the final pages of the Bible, what will we
find God doing? Spending time with His children.
Making His home with them. Being together.

GARY CHAPMAN

4

SET THE SCENE

Celebrate God's constant presence with an unusual
day out. We call it the "Get Lost Date," but it's
really more of a "Random Destination Date."

Rather than heading for a familiar restaurant,
coffee shop, or park, take a road less traveled toward
a destination you know nothing about. Select a
route on a whim, and make an adventure of getting

"lost" together. As you make your way toward an unfamiliar destination, celebrate God's nearness.

MAKE IT HAPPEN

Giving someone instructions on how to get lost seems like an oxymoron. Yet the more creativity you put into the date, the more you'll both enjoy it. One option is to print out a map of your state (or of your county, if you'd prefer to stay closer to home). Close your eyes and mark a point on the map with a pencil. Make that your destination.

Another option is to make up a set of random directions. When you hit the road, try to follow the directions as closely as you can. See where you end up.

Once you reach your destination, explore the surroundings. Walk around. Take in the sights. If you're in a populated area, interact with the locals. See if you can learn something new.

Obviously we can't recommend something as radical as getting lost without following up with some obligatory safety precautions.

- ▶ Follow the *spirit*—but not necessarily the *letter*—of the rules. If your first coordinates lead you to some risky terrain or a dangerous area, alter them. Trust your instincts. If a place doesn't feel right, go somewhere else.

- ▶ Make sure your car is up to the task. Check your gas, tires, and fluids before you get lost. If weather conditions are bad, save this idea for another day.

- ▶ Pack a first-aid kit along with an ample supply of food, water, and blankets.

- Make sure your phones are charged in case of emergency. (Avoid *really* getting lost—use a GPS or map out your return trip home.)

- Once you've sketched out your itinerary, share it with a friend or family member. Make sure someone knows where you're heading and how you're getting there.

FINISH STRONG

Before you end your Get Lost Date, spend a few minutes talking together about the experience and what you'll take away from it. Use the following questions as needed to guide your discussion:

- Were you fearful or apprehensive at all during this date? If so, how did it feel knowing we were together? How does it feel knowing God is always with us?

- Was there anything that surprised you during this date?

- Was there an interesting person we met today who you'll always remember?

MIND YOUR LANGUAGE

If your date's primary love language is Quality Time, make sure your excursion is filled with it. Share with each other times when you felt lost—physically, spiritually, or emotionally. What were the triggers? How did you deal with your feelings? How did the people around you react? How did God make His presence felt during that time? What did you take away from the experience?

TAKE IT TO GOD

Before your date, read David's words in Psalm 139:7 aloud together: "I can never escape from your Spirit! I can never get away from your presence!" Spend some time in prayer, thanking God that what was true for David is true for you, too. Ask God to

- ▶ give you safe travels to and from your destination;
- ▶ bless your efforts to bond with each other;
- ▶ help you develop a deeper appreciation for His continuous presence.

DIG DEEP

Want to check out some more passages that talk about God's continuous presence in the lives of those who serve Him? Try these:

- ▶ Exodus 33:14
- ▶ Joshua 1:9
- ▶ Psalm 16:11
- ▶ Psalm 51:11
- ▶ Psalm 140:13
- ▶ Devotional reading from *The Love Languages Devotional Bible*, page 1346

TO NEXT DATE

THE FACTORY TOUR DATE

WORDS TO GROW ON

You made all the delicate, inner parts of my body and knit me together in my mother's womb. Thank you for making me so wonderfully complex! Your workmanship is marvelous—how well I know it. You watched me as I was being formed in utter seclusion, as I was woven together in the dark of the womb. You saw me before I was born. Every day of my life was recorded in your book. Every moment was laid out before a single day had passed.

PSALM 139:13–16

Our heavenly Father loves us. We can't do anything to increase or decrease our value in His sight.

GARY CHAPMAN

SET THE SCENE

At first glance, a factory tour may seem about as romantic as a tax audit. Yet with a little research—and a certain biblical perspective—your factory tour date could be a rousing success.

Educationally speaking, you might gain a new appreciation for the craftsmanship, technology, and resources used in manufacturing certain products. Spiritually speaking, you might gain a deeper appreciation for the way God has designed you and everyone you encounter. That kind of renewed appreciation could have a remarkable effect on the way you interact with others.

MAKE IT HAPPEN

Obviously, your options for factory tours will depend on your location. If you happen to live in Pennsylvania, scheduling a tour of one of the Hershey Company factories would make for a sweet date. Check the factories in your area for details.

Naturally you'll want to start with things that interest you—say, a jelly bean factory or a Porsche plant. But if you can't do those, don't dismiss other, seemingly less interesting possibilities. Who knows? That tour of the cardboard box factory may turn out to be a high point of your life.

Some manufacturing plants may not offer regular tours but will honor special tour requests. And sometimes knowing the right person can get you a tour that otherwise would be unavailable. Do you know anyone at church, in your family, in the neighborhood, or in your circle of acquaintances who works in a factory or manufacturing plant and would be willing to give you a private tour?

On your way to and from the tour, talk about God's craftsmanship—the way He designed the universe, the earth, nature, and the human body. Imagine what it would have been like to witness, or "tour," the spectacular events of creation we read about in Genesis. What creative act of God would you most want to see?

FINISH STRONG

Before you end your Factory Tour Date, spend a few minutes talking about the experience and what you'll take away from it. Use the following questions as needed to guide your discussion:

- ▶ What was the most interesting thing you learned that you didn't know before the date?

- ▶ While watching the different employees, when did you gain a new appreciation for their craftsmanship?

- ▶ How did reflecting on God's craftsmanship affect your perspective on human creativity while on the tour?

 ## MIND YOUR LANGUAGE

If your date's primary love language is Words of Affirmation, write a list of your favorite ingredients God used to make your date. Obviously your list will include physical attributes that will compliment your significant other's looks. But don't lose sight of the intellectual, emotional, and spiritual ingredients. Do they have a knack for explaining complicated things in easy-to-understand ways? Or the ability to make you laugh after you have had a bad day? Is the person you love a faithful prayer warrior?

TAKE IT TO GOD

When was the last time you came to God in awe of His creation? When was the last time you considered how things in nature work together in ways that defy understanding?

The theme of this date—appreciating how things are made—lends itself to an awestruck prayer time before you take your factory tour. Take turns naming aspects of creation—specifically God's human creation—that amaze you. Thank God for His loving craftsmanship. Ask Him to

- bless your time together;
- help you learn something new during your factory tour;
- guide your interaction with people you meet on the tour;
- help you maintain a constant state of wonder at His creation.

DIG DEEP

In the Bible, God's creation is almost always treated with a sense of wonder and amazement, as you can see in the following passages:

- Genesis 1:27
- Job 33:4
- Psalm 139:13–14
- Jeremiah 1:5

- Ephesians 2:10
- Devotional reading from *The Love Languages Devotional Bible*, page 1329

TO NEXT DATE

THE PLAYGROUND DATE

WORDS TO GROW ON

*Direct your children onto the right path,
and when they are older, they will not leave it.*

PROVERBS 22:6

*Your childhood, pleasant or painful,
is your childhood and stands as history.*

GARY CHAPMAN

6

SET THE SCENE

The author of Proverbs 22:6 understood that our
experiences in childhood often determine the way
we turn out as adults. If you and your date want to
understand each other better, find out more about
your childhoods. What better way is there to do
that than to spend some time together on a school
playground? The playground setting may help spark
memories—some good, some bad—that lead to
potential clues about how you became the people
you are today.

MAKE IT HAPPEN

Uptight adults need not embark on this date. When you hit the playground, it's time to be a kid again. To help make that transition, bring along a basketball, a playground ball (for kickball, foursquare, dodgeball, or ball tag), a jump rope, sidewalk chalk, or any other recess accessory you can think of. And then . . . do what kids do.

Chase each other around the monkey bars. Race to the top of the jungle gym. See how long you can hold hands while swinging. And while you're doing those things, talk.

Talk about your playground experiences as kids. Show each other where you would have been found during recess at your school.

> ▶ Would you have been in the middle of an irrationally competitive kickball game, arguing every call that didn't go your way?

> ▶ Would you have been trying your best to look good, look cool, or be seen with the right people?

> ▶ Would you have been jumping off the swings from dangerous heights?

> ▶ Would you have been enduring the embarrassment of being chosen nearly last for football teams, just for the chance to play?

> ▶ Would you have been walking around by yourself or with a friend?

> ▶ Would you have been the one bullied or the one who was bullying others?

A little transparency on your part will go a long way toward helping your date understand you better. Make sure to encourage openness and transparency by showing genuine interest in what your loved one says, withholding judgment about any less-than-flattering things that are revealed.

FINISH STRONG

Before you end your Playground Date, spend a few minutes talking about the experience and what you'll take away from it. Use the following questions as needed to guide your discussion:

- ▶ Did the memories that were stirred up from your childhood bring you comfort or pain?

- ▶ If they were painful, how can I help you move toward healing?

- ▶ How can we continue to remind each other that we are children of God who are intentionally created and very loved?

 ## MIND YOUR LANGUAGE

How many childhood romances began at recess? Many people had their first kiss on a school playground. If your date's primary love language is Physical Touch, look for a way to re-create that adolescent rite of passage—this time with considerably more experience, considerably less self-consciousness, and, most importantly, no braces to worry about.

If there are other people around, look for little nooks and secluded areas where you can steal a kiss or two. (Married couples may find that those stolen-kiss moments turn into an extremely powerful form of foreplay. If you're all alone, don't worry about seclusion. Go ahead and make out with your spouse anywhere the urge strikes you.)

TAKE IT TO GOD

Before your date, spend some time in prayer together. Thank God for the good memories you have from your childhood. Thank Him for bringing you through the rough patches to make you the person you are today. Ask God to

- ► help you recall memories, good and bad, of childhood;

- ► give you the courage to be transparent about your childhood experiences;

- ► help you both be able to comfort each other if your discussion stirs up unpleasant memories;

- ► develop a deeper appreciation for Him—and for each other.

DIG DEEP

In addition to the words of Proverbs 22:6, the Bible has quite a bit to say about childhood and the transition to adulthood. Here are a few passages to start with:

- ► Deuteronomy 4:9
- ► Deuteronomy 6:6–9
- ► Proverbs 29:17
- ► Ephesians 6:4
- ► 2 Timothy 3:14–15

- ► Devotional reading from *The Love Languages Devotional Bible*, page 1140

THE GEOCACHING DATE

7

WORDS TO GROW ON

*Your word is a lamp to guide my feet
and a light for my path.*

PSALM 119:105

*Our heavenly Father loves us
not because of anything we are or do
but because He created us.*

GARY CHAPMAN

SET THE SCENE

Geocaching is an outdoor treasure hunt in which
players try to find hidden containers using a smartphone or GPS. (For more information, check out
http://www.geocaching.com.) Its appeal as a date
activity is obvious, especially for those who love
the outdoors. The cost is minimal. It can be done
anytime. And it's a great way for you and your date

to work as teammates toward a common goal. The whole thing is just crawling with bonding opportunities.

Chief among them is the chance to talk about "spiritual geocaching"—that is, being directed to the treasure God has waiting for us by His "GPS," the Bible.

MAKE IT HAPPEN

The rules and procedures of geocaching are easy to find online, so we won't go into a lot of detail about them here. Instead, we'll focus on ways to fill the silence with meaningful conversation during your geocaching hunt.

The following list of questions can help get you started, but you need not feel tied to it. Once your discussion gets rolling, let it go where it will. To ensure that it doesn't fizzle out before it gets meaty, be prepared to answer some—or all—of these questions yourself. If you're open and transparent about your feelings and experiences, good and bad, regarding God's Word, your significant other may be inspired to follow suit.

▶ When it comes to "spiritual geocaching"—looking for God's treasure according to the instructions in His Word—what's the treasure? ("Eternal life" is the obvious answer here, understandably, since it's the greatest treasure ever offered. Yet following God's directions for our lives will uncover a host of other treasures along the way, including peace of mind, a sense of purpose, and solid relationships with other spiritual geocachers.)

▶ When you're faced with a problem, a difficult situation, or an important decision, how likely are you to turn to God immediately? (If the answer is, "It depends," what does it depend on? The urgency of the situation? Whether it feels beyond your control?)

▶ What's the biggest challenge in trying to live your life according to the directions in God's Word?

▶ When was the last time you felt God giving you specific directions—whether through prayer, a Bible passage, or advice from a spiritual leader? What happened?

▶ When was the last time you dealt with a problem by following your own instincts or the advice of someone who wasn't looking after your best spiritual interests? What happened?

FINISH STRONG

Before you end your Geocaching Date, spend a few minutes talking about the experience and what you'll take away from it. Use the following questions as needed to guide your discussion:

▶ What did you enjoy most about our Geocaching Date?

▶ How can we help each other be more quick to turn to God and His Word for direction in our lives?

 ## MIND YOUR LANGUAGE

If your date's primary love language is Receiving Gifts—and if geocaching turns into a new hobby for the two of you—shop for some items that will enhance the experience and your time together. You can find any number of smartphone apps designed for geocachers. If you have a little more money to spend, how about a pair of shoes or boots designed to handle different terrains? Or some high-quality sunglasses? Or a distinctive geocaching hat that fits your date's personality? Or matching geocaching T-shirts for the two of you? With a little imagination, you could have fun while filling each other's love tank.

TAKE IT TO GOD

Before your date, spend some time in prayer as a couple. Thank God for the spiritual treasures He's laid out for us—specifically, the sacrificial death and resurrection of His Son. Thank Him for His gift of Scripture, the road map for our lives. Ask Him to

- ▶ bless your time together;
- ▶ give you safe travels;
- ▶ guide your discussion in a way that brings you closer to Him—and to each other.

DIG DEEP

If you're interested in spiritual geocaching, here are a few Bible coordinates to start with:

- ▶ Psalm 25:9
- ▶ Proverbs 2:6–9
- ▶ Proverbs 3:5–6
- ▶ Jeremiah 29:11
- ▶ John 16:13

- ▶ Devotional reading from *The Love Languages Devotional Bible*, page 70

THE SUNRISE DATE

WORDS TO GROW ON

*The faithful love of the Lord never ends!
His mercies never cease. Great is his faithfulness;
his mercies begin afresh each morning.*

LAMENTATIONS 3:22–23

*I am amazed by how many individuals
mess up every new day with yesterday.*

GARY CHAPMAN

8

SET THE SCENE

You don't have to be a morning person to appreciate
the beauty and significance of a sunrise. Every
dawn brings with it a fresh supply of mercies and
blessings from God. On this Sunrise Date, you and
your spouse will be witnesses to the new day as it
breaks. You'll greet the arrival of dawn, marvel at
God's astonishing creation, celebrate His goodness
in providing a new day, and enjoy each other's
company in a romantic setting.

MAKE IT HAPPEN

Granted, all you really need for this date is the largest object in the solar system. But if you want to make the date truly memorable, there are a few things you can do.

1 *Scout locations for the best vista you can find.*
If you're a morning person, check out a few sunrises by yourself in advance of your date. Try to find the best location in your area to view the sunrise. For example, you might look for a nature setting that offers an unobstructed view of the eastern horizon.

2 *Know your meteorology.*
You can find the times for sunrise and sunset at most weather-forecasting sites. (Or, if you're seriously old school, you can consult your personal copy of *The Farmer's Almanac.*) Once you know the time of the sunrise, you can plan your date accordingly.

3 *Adjust your sleep schedule.*
Make sure you both get plenty of rest the night before your Sunrise Date. This is especially important if one (or both) of you is not a morning person. The last thing you want to do is arrive tired and cranky for your date.

4 *Don't show up empty-handed.*
Bring along some coffee . . . doughnuts . . . coffee . . . bagels and cream cheese . . . coffee . . . pastries . . . coffee . . . or perhaps your favorite fast-food breakfast sandwiches. Just don't forget the coffee. For maximum effect, pack a basket

(complete with plates, napkins, utensils, and anything else you might need) and enjoy a picnic breakfast together while you watch the sun rise.

5 *Approach the date with a Psalm 118:24 attitude.*
The verse says, "This is the day the Lord has made. We will rejoice and be glad in it." Reflect that spirit in your interaction with each other. Talk about the sacredness of the new day—and how you can show your joy and gladness for it.

FINISH STRONG

Before you end your Sunrise Date, spend a few minutes talking with each other about the experience and what you'll take away from it. Use the following questions as needed to guide your discussion.

- ▶ Why is it so easy to lose sight of the potential that every new day brings?

- ▶ What does God want us to do with this day?

- ▶ How can we help each other maintain a "Psalm 118:24 attitude"?

MIND YOUR LANGUAGE

If your significant other's primary love language is Gifts, create a memento of your Sunrise Date. As dawn is breaking, take a picture together with the sunrise clearly visible behind you. Print the photo, find the perfect frame for it, and present it to your date, along with a note that says something like, "The sunrise is only the *second* most amazing thing in this photo. Thank you for greeting a new day with me."

TAKE IT TO GOD

Before your Sunrise Date, spend some time in prayer as a couple. Thank God for the coming new day—and for His mercies and blessings that will come with it. Thank Him for letting you greet the new day with your amazing friend. Ask Him to

- ▶ bless your early-morning time together;
- ▶ help you recognize His mercies and blessings throughout the day;
- ▶ help you help others recognize and appreciate the opportunities that a new day brings.

DIG DEEP

If you'd like to read more passages that fit the theme of the Sunrise Date, try these.

- ▶ Judges 21:4
- ▶ Psalm 118:24
- ▶ Malachi 1:11
- ▶ Mark 1:35

- ▶ Luke 1:78
- ▶ Devotional reading from *The Love Languages Devotional Bible*, page 611

TO NEXT DATE

THE WATER DATE

WORDS TO GROW ON

*But those who drink the water I give
will never be thirsty again. It becomes
a fresh, bubbling spring within them,
giving them eternal life.*

JOHN 4:14

*If you are thirsty for a glass of water,
and [someone] offers you a seat to rest upon—
it's nice, but it doesn't quench your thirst.
Similarly, acts of encouragement or
demonstrations of appreciation in ways
that are not meaningful to a [person]
may be appreciated as a nice gesture,
but one's deeper need for appreciation
remains unmet.*

GARY CHAPMAN

9

SET THE SCENE

Water plays a key role in Scripture—as the focus of Days 2 and 3 of creation (Genesis 1:6–13), as the means by which God destroyed almost all life on the planet (Genesis 7:1–24), as the route of escape for the Israelites leaving Egypt (Exodus 14:15–28), as a platform for Jesus' miracles (Matthew 8:23–27; 14:22–33), and as the method of baptism (Matthew 3:13–17). Jesus even referred to Himself as the source of living water (John 7:37–38).

Why not make water the key element of a special date? You can enjoy the pleasure of God's liquid creation while you talk about how God has used water in His dealings with people.

MAKE IT HAPPEN

Water covers more than 70 percent of the planet. Unless you're a desert nomad, you likely have access to a body of water, even if it's just a pond or a creek. Obviously, the kind of date you plan and prepare for will depend on the type of water available to you.

If you live near an ocean, pack for a day at the beach. Bring reading material, comfortable chairs, shovels and pails for building sand castles, and the right footwear for a nice long walk on the beach.

If you live near a river, lake, or reservoir, you might pack fishing equipment or a picnic lunch. If you live near a pond or small creek, you might plan for a hike or nature walk—anything that puts you near the water.

Along with your physical preparation, you'll need to do some biblical preparation. During your date, you'll want to steer your conversation toward stories in the Bible that feature water. In order to do that naturally, you'll need to familiarize yourself with those stories.

Several examples (and their corresponding passages) are listed in the "Set the Scene" section above, including:

- ► Creation
- ► The Flood
- ► The Israelites Crossing the Red Sea
- ► Jesus Calming the Storm at Sea
- ► Jesus Walking on the Surface of the Water
- ► Jesus' Baptism

Talk about how you picture those incidents and what it must have been like to witness them. Let your date be filled with a sense of awe and amazement at God's might.

FINISH STRONG

Before you end your Water Date, spend a few minutes talking about the experience. Use the following questions as needed to guide your discussion.

- ► Why is water such an amazing part of God's creation?
- ► What does water tell us about God?
- ► What difference is Jesus' living water making in our lives?
- ► How can we use the memories of this date—and our discussion of God's might—the next time we face a crisis?

MIND YOUR LANGUAGE

If your significant other's primary language is Acts of Service, make sure you pack two separate bags for the trip—one for you and one for your date. Do your best to think of all the things you both could possibly need for your Water Date—a change of clothes, a favorite fishing hat, or snacks.

TAKE IT TO GOD

Before your Water Date, spend some time in prayer as a couple. Praise God for the beauty of His creation, especially as it pertains to water. Thank Him for the role water plays in our daily lives. Ask God to

- ▶ keep you safe during your Water Date;
- ▶ bless your time together so that you will bring honor to Him;
- ▶ help you develop a renewed appreciation for the living water Jesus offers.

DIG DEEP

The Bible contains several passages that talk about water. Here's a small sampling.

- ▶ Exodus 14:21–22
- ▶ Psalm 23:1–2
- ▶ Isaiah 43:2
- ▶ John 3:5
- ▶ Revelation 22:1

- ▶ Devotional reading from *The Love Languages Devotional Bible*, page 1064

TO NEXT DATE

THE 5K DATE

WORDS TO GROW ON

*Don't you realize that in a race everyone runs,
but only one person gets the prize? So run to win!
All athletes are disciplined in their training.
They do it to win a prize that will fade away,
but we do it for an eternal prize. So I run with
purpose in every step. I am not just shadowboxing.
I discipline my body like an athlete, training it
to do what it should. Otherwise, I fear that after
preaching to others I myself might be disqualified.*

1 CORINTHIANS 9:24–27

*[Real] love requires effort and discipline.
It is the choice to expend energy in an effort
to benefit the other person, knowing that if his
or her life is enriched by your effort, you too
will find a sense of satisfaction—the satisfaction
of having genuinely loved another.*

GARY CHAPMAN

SET THE SCENE

You don't have to be an elite athlete to complete a 5k race. You don't even necessarily have to like running. All you need is a goal, the drive to achieve it, and a partner who will help you see it through.

That's why the 5k Date—and the training that goes with it—can be a challenging but fulfilling date. Completing the race is a goal you can work toward together. Along the way, you'll likely experience peaks and valleys—feelings of accomplishment and frustration. But hopefully the thrill of crossing the finish line—together—will be worth it and may prove to be a building block in your relationship.

MAKE IT HAPPEN

If you decide to embark on this 5k Date, make sure you treat it seriously. Decide whether you both want to run or walk the course, and set a time goal for yourselves—something to aim for and work toward.

Ideally your 5k Date will be a *series* of dates. If your schedule allows, plan to train together at least two or three times a week in the months leading up to the 5k race. The more you train, the more confident you'll feel on race day. The more confident you feel, the better your date will be.

Here are some tips for making your 5k Date a pleasant experience for both of you.

1 *Be reasonable.*
If you're a particularly competitive person, you could set up a training regimen to help you beat your personal best time. But

remember, this is a date, not a Nike commercial. Set a goal that makes sense, based on who is the least in shape of the two of you.

2 Keep things fun and upbeat.
As you prepare for the 5k, keep your ultracompetitive instincts in check. Be generous with your praise and encouragement. Celebrate your date's tiniest victories and smallest bits of progress.

3 Togetherness is the key.
Once again, this isn't about individual glory. Your goal should be to run the race together, stride for stride, all the way to the finish line.

FINISH STRONG

After the race, grab a coffee or a smoothie and spend time talking about the experience. Use the following questions as needed to guide your discussion.

- ▶ What did we learn about ourselves as a couple from this date?

- ▶ How can we apply that to other areas of our lives and our relationship?

- ▶ What's the next challenge we can tackle together using our God-given skills and motivation?

 ## MIND YOUR LANGUAGE

If you're married and your spouse's primary love language is Physical Touch, offer a massage after each training session. For maximum effect, consult massage books and websites for tips on how to target specific muscles. If you're single, give your date a relaxing foot rub to celebrate his or her accomplishment.

TAKE IT TO GOD

Before your 5k Date—that is, the race day itself —spend some time in prayer as a couple. Thank God for giving you bodies that are capable of completing a 5k race. Ask Him to

- keep you safe and injury-free throughout the race;
- bless your efforts to shape, train, and improve your body—that is, His temple;
- accept all the glory for your accomplishment.

DIG DEEP

Here are some additional passages you can use for motivation during your 5k Date.

- Psalm 37:23–24
- Isaiah 40:31
- Matthew 19:26
- Philippians 4:13

- Colossians 3:23–24
- Devotional reading from *The Love Languages Devotional Bible*, page 783

TO NEXT DATE

DESIGN-A-SHIRT DATE

WORDS TO GROW ON

The Lord has filled Bezalel with the Spirit of God, giving him great wisdom, ability, and expertise in all kinds of crafts.

EXODUS 35:31

Humans are instinctively creative. . . . We are made in the image of a God who creates, and we who bear His image have tremendous creative potential.

GARY CHAPMAN

11

SET THE SCENE

If you attended camp as a youngster or spent some time in a church youth group, you may have some experience in making T-shirts. But how much creative input did you have—beyond, say, choosing the colors for your tie-dye? How accurately did the finished product reflect your creativity and vision?

Here's a chance to express yourself a little more fully through fashion design—and perhaps to learn something new about your spouse in the process. Let your artistic impulses run wild as you create a shirt to wear on a date with your spouse.

MAKE IT HAPPEN

The Design-a-Shirt Date is actually a two-stage date. The first stage is the design process. This is where you let you imaginations run wild as you decorate plain shirts according to your individual style. T-shirts are certainly the easiest and cheapest to decorate, but any kind of shirt will work.

The style of decorating you choose, whether it's iron-on, permanent markers, painting, or applique, will determine the supplies you need. Make sure you keep plenty of extras (including T-shirts) on hand, in case of mistakes.

Put some thought and effort into your creation. Make sure the shirt you design says something about you. For example, you might put your favorite nickname on the back, jersey-style. You might paint things (or iron on patches) that represent your favorite hobbies or interests. You might fill the shirt with some of your favorite quotes. Anything that reveals something about you is an option.

Don't work in silence, though. Talk about your ideas. Pay each other compliments. Encourage each other, especially if ideas that seemed doable at first turn out not to be. Keep the stress level low. Make it an enjoyable time together.

The second stage of the date—which probably won't take place on the same day as the first stage because of the time needed for the shirts to dry—is to wear your shirts in public.

Plan a casual outing of bowling, miniature golf, or a picnic—anything in which a homemade T-shirt would be considered appropriate attire. Be prepared to compliment your spouse on his or her design skills—and to field questions from curious passersby.

FINISH STRONG

Before you end your Design-a-Shirt Date, spend a few minutes talking with your spouse about the experience. Use the following questions as needed to guide your discussion.

- ▶ How comfortable are you when it comes to expressing your creativity and individuality?

- ▶ What are some of the obstacles that get in the way of healthy expressions of creativity and individuality?

- ▶ What specific steps can you take to celebrate and encourage one another's creativity and uniqueness?

MIND YOUR LANGUAGE

If your spouse's primary love language is Physical Touch, make sure you provide plenty of it throughout the date. During the design process, occasionally place your hand on your spouse's hand or rub her back—a little something to let her know how you feel. The trying-on process will give you plenty of opportunities to lovingly smooth the wrinkles in your spouse's shirt with your hands. Take advantage of them.

TAKE IT TO GOD

Before your date, spend some time in prayer with your spouse. Thank God for the fact that you are created in His image—specifically for the fact that you have the ability to create, as He does. Thank Him for the creativity and individuality you see in your spouse. Ask God to

- ▶ bless your time with your spouse during your Design-a-Shirt Date

- ▶ help you maintain a spirit of fun, creativity, and good-naturedness for the duration of your date

- ▶ come away from your date with a renewed thankfulness and appreciation for your spouse's creativity and uniqueness.

DIG DEEP

The Bible encourages us to express our God-given creativity and unique personality. Here are a few passages that fit the theme of expressing ourselves.

- ▶ Romans 12:6–8
- ▶ Ephesians 2:10
- ▶ Colossians 3:23
- ▶ 1 Timothy 4:14

- ▶ 1 Peter 4:10–11
- ▶ Devotional reading from *The Love Languages Devotional Bible*, page 245

TO NEXT DATE

THE SPIRITUAL HERITAGE DATE

WORDS TO GROW ON

Therefore, since we are surrounded by such a huge crowd of witnesses to the life of faith, let us strip off every weight that slows us down, especially the sin that so easily trips us up. And let us run with endurance the race God has set before us.

HEBREWS 12:1

Take the time to explore the history and beliefs of your religious heritage and discuss your journey openly with the person you are dating.

GARY CHAPMAN

SET THE SCENE

The title of this date may not scream, "Excitement!" or "Romance!" but it has the potential to be a game changer in your relationship. If you want to develop spiritual intimacy with your spouse or significant other, look to his or her spiritual heritage—not just what they believe, but how they came to those beliefs.

What role did his family play? Who were her spiritual mentors? At what points did he get off track? Who brought her back?

What better environment is there for a conversation about spiritual heritage than a church in your area that's been around for years—a place with its own rich spiritual heritage? On this date, tour an old church building and learn about its history while you learn about each other's spiritual history.

MAKE IT HAPPEN

For your Spiritual Heritage Date, look for a church in your area that's not just old, but one that has a rich history as well. Depending on where you live, you might look for a church that was part of the Underground Railroad or one that was instrumental in the civil rights movement. Or you might look for a church that was home to a respected leader or historical figure.

If you're unsure about the legacies of the churches in your area, talk to someone at your local historical society. If you have time, you may want to explore more than one church on your date.

If you have a chance to plan the date in advance, call the office of the church you plan to visit. Explain what you're doing and see if you can get a guided tour of the building. You might even want to do some online research about the church so that you're prepared to ask relevant questions.

When you're alone with each other, talk about the spiritual heritage of the church. Do you suppose current members feel compelled to live up to that legacy? Spend some time talking about your own spiritual heritage as well. Do you ever feel pressure to live up to the example of those who mentored you? If so, is that a good thing or a bad thing?

FINISH STRONG

Before you end your Spiritual Heritage Date, talk about the experience with each other. Use the following questions as needed to guide your discussion.

- ▶ How would having a spiritual mentor affect your everyday decision making?
- ▶ What are the qualities of a good spiritual mentor?
- ▶ What steps can we take to become more effective spiritual mentors?

MIND YOUR LANGUAGE

If your date's primary love language is Quality Time, be prepared to ask some probing questions about his or her spiritual heritage. Listen intently to your date's answers. Encourage him or her to open up. Let the rest of the world go by. Keep your attention focused on what they are saying for as long as they care to talk.

TAKE IT TO GOD

Before your date, spend some time in prayer as a couple. Thank God for the spiritual mentors who have passed on and become a cloud of witnesses. Thank Him for the spiritual mentors who are currently making a difference in your life. Ask Him to help you

- ▶ open up to each other on your Spiritual Heritage Date;
- ▶ express your gratitude and appreciation to the spiritual mentors in your life;
- ▶ become spiritual mentors to others.

DIG DEEP

Several other Scripture passages emphasize the importance of spiritual mentors—people who encourage us to be all God intends us to be. Here are a few of them.

- ▶ Psalm 119:130
- ▶ Proverbs 27:17
- ▶ 2 Timothy 2:2
- ▶ Titus 2:3–5

- ▶ 1 Peter 5:1–5
- ▶ Devotional reading from *The Love Languages Devotional Bible*, page 542

TO NEXT DATE

THE HONEYDEW DATE

WORDS TO GROW ON

*Two people are better off than one,
for they can help each other succeed.
If one person falls, the other can reach out
and help. But someone who falls alone
is in real trouble. Likewise, two people
lying close together can keep each
other warm. But how can one be warm alone?
A person standing alone can be attacked
and defeated, but two can stand back-to-back
and conquer. Three are even better,
for a triple-braided cord is not easily broken.*

ECCLESIASTES 4:9–12

*A husband and wife come together
with their differences to form a team
where each will use his or her strengths
to help the other, and together they will use their
abilities to make the world a better place.*

GARY CHAPMAN

13

SET THE SCENE

The Honeydew Date is the very definition of enjoying the best of both worlds. On the one hand, you have the opportunity to spend quality time with your significant other, working together and basking in each other's company. On the other hand, you have a chance to complete some long-neglected tasks and cross some errands off your to-do list.

The key to success on this date is keeping your priorities in the right order. Job #1 is to enjoy time as a couple. Job #2 is to get things done.

MAKE IT HAPPEN

Obviously your date will be shaped by the jobs you choose to tackle together. Here are some tips to help make your Honeydew Date memorable.

1 *If you don't have a to-do list already written, write one.*
Don't just move from one job to another as they occur to you. Make a master list of things you want to get done. Treat yourselves to the sense of accomplishment that comes from crossing things off the list.

2 *Remember: ambitious yet manageable.*
Take stock of the time you have available for your Honeydew Date and choose tasks you can complete in that time. Don't overbook yourselves. The last thing you want is to finish

the date feeling frustrated with what you *didn't* get done, instead of feeling good about what you *did* accomplish together.

3 *Honor seniority.*
If possible, tackle the task that's been on your to-do list longer than any of the others. You'll find there's something genuinely satisfying about completing a job that's been hanging over your head forever.

4 *Don't forget to dance.*
Create a music playlist for your Honeydew Date. Sprinkle it liberally with your date's favorite artists. Take some time out of your workday to dance—or if you're married, to have some other kind of fun.

5 *Treats are always nice.*
Surprise your hardworking honey with his or her favorite break-time snack. Reward yourselves with ice cream at the end of your date to celebrate your accomplishments.

6 *Talk about your teamwork.*
Pay attention to the way the two of you work together. Bring attention to your date's work ethic, attention to detail, and many other strengths. Talk about the way the two of you complement each other's work style.

FINISH STRONG

Before you end your Honeydew Date, talk with your spouse about the experience. Use the following questions as needed to guide your discussion.

- Ecclesiastes 4:12 says, "A triple-braided cord is not easily broken." How does that apply to our relationship?
- What makes us such a good team?
- What could God accomplish through us?

MIND YOUR LANGUAGE

If your sweetheart's primary love language is Acts of Service, choose the item on your list that's closest to his or her heart—perhaps organizing his tool bench or cleaning her car—and tackle that one first.

TAKE IT TO GOD

Before your date, spend some time in prayer together. Thank God for bringing you together as teammates and coworkers. Thank Him for the fact that your relationship is more than just the sum of its individual parts—for the fact that together you form something special, something valuable, and something productive. Ask Him to help you

- maintain a balance between fun and productivity during your date;
- deepen your relationship with each other;
- establish a sense of teamwork and cooperation that will last long after your Honeydew Date.

DIG DEEP

Want to check out some more passages that talk about the importance of working together? Try these.

- Proverbs 27:17
- Matthew 18:20
- Colossians 3:23
- Hebrews 10:24–25

- Devotional reading from *The Love Languages Devotional Bible*, page 987

TO NEXT DATE

THE DOUBLE DATE

WORDS TO GROW ON

*Don't be fooled by those who say such things,
for "bad company corrupts good character."*

1 CORINTHIANS 15:33

Intimacy *is the word used to describe
a close relationship. Intimacy is also one
of our deepest emotional needs. It is the
language of friendship.*

GARY CHAPMAN

SET THE SCENE

Spending time with good friends—reliving past
glories, sharing jokes, talking about anything
and everything—is one of life's greatest pleasures.
Incorporating those friendships into your
marriage, though, can be a tricky proposition.
Many couples opt for the individual route.
She hangs with her friends; he hangs with his.
But there's a better option.

Wise couples learn to build friendships *together* with other couples. One of the best ways to do that is by double dating. Friendships are built in a relaxed, casual atmosphere—free from distractions and interruptions. A double date can provide just such an atmosphere.

MAKE IT HAPPEN

If you've already thought of a couple you'd like to spend some time with, take the initiative by inviting them out. If not, brainstorm some potential candidates at church, at work, in the neighborhood, or elsewhere.

Obviously the details of your evening will vary according to your interests and the options available to you. Here are some tips that can tilt the odds of enjoying a memorable Double Date in your favor.

1 *Do a little preparation.*
Before your date, talk about the couple you'll be going out with. Share what you know about their family, careers, background, interests, and hobbies. Look for common ground to build on. Identify potential conversation starters—as well as topics to avoid. A little preparation can go a long way toward reducing awkward silences.

2 *Avoid controversial topics.*
You know how it is. One statement can ignite a debate that torches your entire evening. Some people are extremely passionate about their beliefs—and vehement about defending them. Among longtime friends, that's not necessarily a problem. Over time, you learn how to agree to disagree—or how to defuse a tense situation with a joke.

With people you don't know well, you may not have those options. Your best bet then is to avoid hot-button topics—at least until you get to know each other better.

3 *Avoid pairing off.*
Keep in mind that a double date isn't the time for "girl talk" or "guy talk." For one thing, one of you may not be as comfortable as the other with the person he or she is paired with, which may lead to awkwardness and annoyance. For another, a double date is a time for you both, as a couple, to form friendships *together*. As much as possible, make sure your conversations are group efforts.

4 *Don't forget your date.*
A double date is still a date. The fact that other people are with you shouldn't change anything between you and your honey. Show your partner the love, affection, attention, and respect you would show if it were just the two of you.

FINISH STRONG

After your Double Date, when you're alone, talk about the experience. Use the following questions as needed to guide your discussion.

- ▶ What can we tell about the other couple, based on our time together?

- ▶ What can they tell about us?

- ▶ Could they see Christ in us? If so, how?

MIND YOUR LANGUAGE

If your significant other's primary love language is Words of Affirmation, look for opportunities during your Double Date to sing their praises. For example, if the conversation leads to how marriage or dating has changed you, you could talk about how your sweetheart has helped you

- ▶ slow down;
- ▶ look at things from a different perspective;
- ▶ laugh more;
- ▶ feel good about yourself.

TAKE IT TO GOD

Before your Double Date, spend some time in prayer together. Start by praising God for bringing people into your lives who genuinely care about you. Thank Him for the opportunity to go out with your friends. Ask Him to help you

- ▶ steer the conversation in a way that pleases Him;
- ▶ strike a good balance between listening and talking;
- ▶ deal patiently with the other couple's petty annoyances and idiosyncrasies—and help them patiently deal with yours.

DIG DEEP

The following passages shed light on the importance of maintaining friendships.

- ▸ Proverbs 12:26
- ▸ Proverbs 13:20
- ▸ Proverbs 22:24–25
- ▸ Luke 6:31

- ▸ Romans 12:10
- ▸ Devotional reading from *The Love Languages Devotional Bible*, page 16

TO NEXT DATE

THE CANOE DATE

WORDS TO GROW ON

*May God, who gives this patience and
encouragement, help you live in complete
harmony with each other, as is fitting for
followers of Christ Jesus.*

ROMANS 15:5

*The antidote to divorce is to stop the process of
drifting apart. Choose to paddle your canoes toward
each other, rather than away from each other.*

GARY CHAPMAN

SET THE SCENE

A canoe is a floating microcosm of a close relationship. You've got two people in the same boat, each
equipped to move the vessel. Sometimes they glide
through perfectly calm waters together. Sometimes
they are carried along by strong currents. Sometimes
they are buffeted by waves. And sometimes they
must make their way against the stream.

When they work together, heading toward the same destination, they can make their way through any conditions. When they try to work separately or head in different directions, things get unstable.

To illustrate the point—and to enjoy some time on the water together—plan a canoe trip for two.

MAKE IT HAPPEN

If you decide to pursue a Canoe Date, you'll need to do your homework—especially if one or both of you is a canoeing rookie. Remember, nothing spoils a romantic mood quicker than a life-threatening emergency—or a few hours spent in wet clothes.

Here are a few tips to help you plan an outing that you and your date will remember—fondly, that is.

1 *Find the right water for your skill level.*
If you have little experience in a canoe, stay away from whitewater rapids, stretches with rocky obstacles, and long runs that will try your endurance (and patience). Remember, this isn't an Outward Bound expedition; it's a date.

2 *Always wear your life jacket.*
A canoe can tip over at any time. Make sure that if you go into the water, you're equipped with a flotation device. Even strong swimmers can get in trouble in unfamiliar waters.

3 *Pay attention to the currents.*
Don't let the water carry you farther downstream than you planned. If you feel yourself being pulled faster than you're comfortable, paddle toward the shore.

4 *Tie your equipment to the canoe.*
You'll want to bring plenty of food and water, a first-aid kit, sun protection, a map, a phone, an extra set of dry clothes—as well as a waterproof bag to hold it all. Tie the bag to a center beam in the canoe so you won't lose everything if the canoe tips over.

FINISH STRONG

Before you end your Canoe Date, spend a few minutes talking about the experience and what you'll take away from it. Use the following questions as needed to guide your discussion.

▶ When was the last time we "paddled together" in dealing with a situation or circumstance in our relationship? What were the results?

▶ When was the last time we paddled separately? What were the results?

▶ If our relationship is a canoe, how can we keep it pointed in the direction God wants us to go?

 ## MIND YOUR LANGUAGE

If your significant other's primary love language is Words of Affirmation, spend some time on the water talking about what a difference it's made in your life to be in the same "boat" as your date. Be as specific as possible in your affirmation.

Keeping the date theme in mind, you might share how your significant other has

▶ offered a steadying hand when things got a little shaky;

- pointed you in the right direction when you got turned around;

- paddled for the both of you on occasion.

TAKE IT TO GOD

Before your Canoe Date, spend some time in prayer together. Thank God for the privilege of sharing a "boat" with your significant other on the river of life. Ask Him to

- bless the time you spend together on your Canoe Date;

- give you safe travels;

- help you work together as partners, keeping your boat pointed in the right direction.

DIG DEEP

If you'd like to read more passages that fit the theme of the Canoe Date, try these.

- Genesis 2:18

- Proverbs 27:17

- Ecclesiastes 4:9–10

- 1 Corinthians 1:10

- Hebrews 10:24–25

- Devotional reading from *The Love Languages Devotional Bible*, page 728

TO NEXT DATE

THE SERVICE DATE

WORDS TO GROW ON

*Let us think of ways to motivate one another
to acts of love and good works.*

HEBREWS 10:24

*Service to others is the highest pinnacle
humanity ever scales.*

GARY CHAPMAN

16

SET THE SCENE

Christians are the body of Christ on earth. Each
part of that body has unique features—God-given
gifts and abilities—that allow us to accomplish
God's will. One part of the body, working solo, can
accomplish much. Two parts of the body, working
together, can accomplish much more.

That's the reasoning behind the Service Date.
If you're married, God brought you and your spouse
together for a purpose beyond romance. He brought
you together to serve Him. By combining the skills

and abilities He's given you in a way that complements each other, you can increase your ministry potential.

MAKE IT HAPPEN

There is no shortage of ministry opportunities available to you because there is no shortage of people in need. Here are some tips for making your Service Date a memorable experience for you—and, more importantly, a helpful experience for the people you serve.

1 *Understand your options.*
Get in touch with the outreach ministry in your church. Talk to the ministry leaders about what you have to offer, whether it's particular skills or a willingness to do whatever is asked of you. See what pressing ministry needs they have.

2 *Get off the sidelines.*
When it comes to service, there are no experts or rookies —only those who do and those who watch (or *talk* about doing). Be a doer. Find out what needs to be done—whether it's washing dishes, clearing an area of trash and debris, or entertaining a group of toddlers—and jump in. If there are things you need to know, other volunteers will help you. Just make sure you learn on the job.

3 *Watch each other in action.*
If married, fix an image in your mind of your spouse serving or interacting with someone in need. The next time you grow frustrated with your spouse, when you're tempted to think the worst of her, recall that image. Don't lose sight of who she really is.

4 *Think in terms of permanence.*
Maybe the service opportunity you choose will prove to be a perfect fit for you both. If so, build it into your weekly schedule ASAP. Make yourselves an integral part of the ministry —and make the ministry an integral part of your life.

FINISH STRONG

Before you end your Service Date, spend a few minutes talking to each other about the experience and its effects on you. Use the following questions as needed to guide your discussion.

- ▶ What difference did we make in someone else's life today?

- ▶ What difference did we make in our lives today?

- ▶ How can we "motivate one another to acts of love and good works"?

MIND YOUR LANGUAGE

If you're married and your spouse's primary love language is Acts of Service, take advantage of the opportunity to gain some much-needed service experience. Commit yourself to taking on one of your spouse's primary chores or household tasks every week—preferably, a different chore each week. For example, one week you might cook Sunday dinner; the next week you might pick up the kids from practice.

If your spouse asks what you're doing, just say you're practicing your serving skills. Give thanks to God for the fact that you can make a real difference in your spouse's life simply by completing a task.

TAKE IT TO GOD

Before your date, spend some time together in prayer. Praise God for the fact that He has a special place in His heart for the poor and needy. Thank Him for giving you the opportunity to serve Him as you serve others. Ask Him to

- ▶ help you keep a proper perspective about your service—specifically, to help you keep an attitude of humility;

- ▶ give you the chance to interact on a meaningful level with the people you're serving—to make a difference in their lives and let them make a difference in yours;

- ▶ open your eyes to the gifts and abilities you have to offer people in need.

DIG DEEP

The Bible is filled with passages that talk about serving others. Here's a small sampling.

- ▶ John 13:12–14
- ▶ Acts 20:35
- ▶ Galatians 5:13–14
- ▶ Philippians 2:1–11

- ▶ 1 Peter 4:10
- ▶ Devotional reading from *The Love Languages Devotional Bible*, page 1241

TO NEXT DATE

THE PICNIC DATE

WORDS TO GROW ON

*But Jesus often withdrew to the
wilderness for prayer.*

LUKE 5:16

*Finding a time and a place may be difficult
in our fast-paced world, but the heart that
longs for God will make time for Him.*

GARY CHAPMAN

17

SET THE SCENE

Forget the clichés you've seen in movies or cartoons.
This Picnic Date is about more than eating baked
beans and potato salad from flimsy paper plates.
The Picnic Date is about getting away from the
noisy interruptions of everyday life and retreating
to a place of quiet solitude. It's about following
Jesus' example.

Jesus regularly retreated to a quiet place to
pray (see the passages in "Dig Deep"). The solitude

refreshed and recharged Him. Imagine what a quiet retreat could do for you and your significant other.

MAKE IT HAPPEN

A well-packed basket can mean the difference between a good Picnic Date and a great one. Toward that end, this date would be the perfect time to remember some of each other's favorite food and drink items—even the ones that may have been mentioned only once or twice. When you unpack a can of his favorite (hard-to-find) peach soda, you'll set an ideal tone for the date.

Make sure you cover other bases as well. Did you pack the necessary condiments? How about plates, utensils, and napkins? Mosquito spray? The more contingencies you plan for, the better your chances of success.

Look for a picnic site that's fairly isolated—a place that will help you feel removed from the pressures and distractions of everyday life. Spend time communing with God and each other in nature.

Observe and interact with your surroundings. Depending on the location and time of year, you might

- ▶ observe an anthill. It's a picnic; there have to be ants nearby. Watch them go about their business;

- ▶ take up birdwatching. Bring two sets of binoculars and see how many different varieties of birds you can spot (or hear);

- ▶ collect leaves. Bring along a guidebook from the library on trees and leaves and see how many different types you can identify.

As part of your effort to disconnect from the demands and diversions of everyday life, declare certain topics off-limits. Instead, focus on the sights all around you. Talk about the everyday wonders of creation—the seemingly unimportant things that get overlooked amid the seemingly important things in life.

FINISH STRONG

After the picnic, spend a little time talking about the experience. Use the following questions as needed to guide your discussion.

► Why is quiet and solitude important in our Christian walk?

► Why is it important in our relationship?

► What are we willing to sacrifice in order to spend more time together in quiet, secluded settings?

MIND YOUR LANGUAGE

If you're married and your spouse's primary love language is Physical Touch, look for opportunities to make meaningful contact throughout your Picnic Date. For example:

► Sit back against a tree; invite your spouse to sit next to you and put her head on your shoulder. Gently stroke her hair while you enjoy the beauty of God's creation together.

► Ask him to give you a piggyback ride across a shallow stream.

► Take a hike hand in hand.

Better yet, do all of the above. Make sure your significant other returns from your date reenergized, recharged, and with a full love tank.

 ## TAKE IT TO GOD

Before you dig into your picnic food, spend some time in prayer together. Thank God for

► His provisions;

► the beauty of His creation;

► the opportunity to enjoy time with each other in a relaxed setting.

Ask God to bless your time and help you both come away from your Picnic Date with recharged batteries and a renewed appreciation for His creation.

DIG DEEP

Here are some additional passages you can use for your Picnic Date.

► Mark 1:12–13

► Mark 1:35

► Luke 5:16

► Luke 6:12–13

► Luke 11:1–2

► Devotional reading from *The Love Languages Devotional Bible*, page 1280

TO NEXT DATE

THE HOME TOUR DATE

18

WORDS TO GROW ON

A house is built by wisdom and becomes strong through good sense. Through knowledge its rooms are filled with all sorts of precious riches and valuables.

PROVERBS 24:3–4

Love begins, or should begin, at home.

GARY CHAPMAN

SET THE SCENE

What makes a house a home? That question lies at the heart of the Home Tour Date. To answer the question, you and your spouse will walk through homes in your area that open themselves to visitors, usually for a small price. On your tour, you'll take in the sights and sounds of a variety of homes. You're not just looking for decorating tips, though. You're looking for clues into the inner workings of the families who live there.

Ideally your experiences in other people's houses will give you insight into what you appreciate—and what you'd like to change—about your home.

MAKE IT HAPPEN

You can find information about the times, locations, and cost of home tours in your area in your local newspaper or online. Most tours are offered on weekends, so you may want to plan accordingly.

If you're in the market for a new home, this date may serve practical, as well as romantic purposes. Granted, many of the homes featured on these tours are prohibitively expensive, but you may have your eyes opened to locations in your area that you hadn't considered before. Even if you're not in the market for a new house, you may be inspired by some of the homes you see. You might get some ideas for rearranging or redecorating your own place.

More than anything else, though, pay attention to the *feel* of the houses you tour. Look at the pictures on the wall. What stories do they tell? Look at the surroundings. What themes are most prominent in the decorating and furnishings? Does the place feel like just a house—or is it a home? How can you tell?

FINISH STRONG

Before you end your Home Tour Date, spend a few minutes talking with your spouse about the experience. Use the following questions as needed to guide your discussion.

▶ What conclusions might people draw about us, based on our home?

- Do we have a home that honors God?
- What specific changes should we consider in our home?

MIND YOUR LANGUAGE

If your spouse's primary love language is Words of Affirmation, take the opportunity after you leave each open house to tell your spouse what you appreciate about his contributions to your home. Without denigrating the house you just left, share some reasons why you prefer your house—especially reasons that involve your spouse.

For example, you might say, "The dimensions of that garage were bigger than ours; but I think our garage looks bigger because of the way you've organized it. I really appreciate your organizational skills."

TAKE IT TO GOD

Before your date, spend some time in prayer with your spouse. If you grew up in a good home, surrounded by a loving family, thank God for that. If you grew up in a dysfunctional home, thank Him for the power He gives to break the chain of dysfunction. Thank Him for the amazing things He's done—and the amazing things He's going to do—in your relationship with your spouse. Ask Him to

- guard your hearts against envy as you tour other people's homes
- give you a renewed sense of appreciation for your own home

- help you come away with new insights on how to foster a home environment that honors him.

DIG DEEP

If you're looking for more passages that talk about a God-honoring home, try these.

- Joshua 24:15
- Proverbs 3:33
- Proverbs 14:1
- Isaiah 32:18

- Luke 10:38
- Devotional reading from *The Love Languages Devotional Bible*, page 370

TO NEXT DATE

THE SPONTANEOUS DATE

WORDS TO GROW ON

*Wherever your treasure is, there the desires
of your heart will also be.*

LUKE 12:34

*How do we make time? By eliminating
some of the good things we are doing so
that we will have time for the best.*

GARY CHAPMAN

19

SET THE SCENE

The underlying theme of the Spontaneous Date
is priorities. Many people give lip service to the
notion of having their priorities straight. Yet their
actions don't reflect it. Priorities are *revealed*, not
announced. Your top priority is the area of your life
that receives the most quality time and attention.

Some daily responsibilities are inescapable,
of course. Most careers require forty-plus-hour
workweeks. To try to radically alter that would be

irresponsible. Once in a while, though, it's a good idea to do something that lets your significant other know how you would *really* like to spend your time—something like a Spontaneous Date.

MAKE IT HAPPEN

It may seem like an oxymoron, but a successful Spontaneous Date requires some strategic planning. You'll need to choose the day and time carefully. You don't want to compete with a looming deadline or an important meeting on the other person's calendar.

If you have a good relationship with your significant other's boss or coworkers, talk to them about your plan. Find out what day would be best on their calendar to be spontaneously whisked away.

Announce your Spontaneous Date as stealthily or as dramatically as you wish. One possibility would be to arrange for your significant other's boss to call your date personally as they are preparing for work in the morning to tell them not to come in—and to spend the day with you instead. A more dramatic option would be to walk into their office unannounced, grab their hand, and tell them to follow you.

What you choose to do on your Spontaneous Date is secondary to the fact that you're spending time together when you ordinarily wouldn't. Go to a ball game. Hike a trail in a state park. Catch an afternoon matinee. Head for your favorite restaurant. Or—if you're married—spend the afternoon in your bedroom.

All that matters is that you're together, doing something you both enjoy.

FINISH STRONG

Before you end your Spontaneous Date, talk about the experience with each other. Use the following questions as needed to guide your discussion.

- ▶ Do you ever feel as though our relationship is in a rut?
- ▶ Do you ever feel as though our Christian walk is in a rut?
- ▶ Beyond another Spontaneous Date, what can we do to keep things fresh?

MIND YOUR LANGUAGE

If your significant other's primary love language is Quality Time, make that your primary focus during your Spontaneous Date. For example, you might explain your inspiration for the date in this way:

I realized that I spend too much time not doing the thing I want to do most—that is, to spend time with you. I know that can't always be helped. Our schedules get crazy sometimes. But I can do something about it today, so I am. For the rest of the day, it's going to be just you and me.

Obviously it will be much more meaningful if you add your own details, but you get the idea.

TAKE IT TO GOD

Before you embark on your Spontaneous Date, spend a few minutes in prayer as a couple.

Thank God for the freedom you have to spend time with each other. Ask Him to help you

- approach the date with an adventurous, open-to-anything attitude;

- identify areas of your relationship that could use some spontaneity;

- identify elements of your Christian walk that have become stale and routine.

DIG DEEP

Several other Scripture passages emphasize the importance of maintaining God-honoring priorities. Here are a few of them.

- Deuteronomy 6:5
- Matthew 6:33
- Luke 12:22–34
- Romans 12:2

- 1 Timothy 3:5
- Devotional reading from *The Love Languages Devotional Bible*, page 693

TO NEXT DATE

THE KARAOKE DATE

WORDS TO GROW ON

*So I recommend having fun, because there is
nothing better for people in this world than to eat,
drink, and enjoy life. That way they will
experience some happiness along with all the
hard work God gives them under the sun.*

ECCLESIASTES 8:15

*Togetherness has to do with focused attention.
It is giving someone your undivided attention.
As humans, we have a fundamental desire to
connect with others. We may be in the presence
of people all day long, but we do not
always feel connected.*

GARY CHAPMAN

SET THE SCENE

Are you an extrovert? Do you enjoy being the center
of attention? Do you live for applause? Are you willing
to risk your reputation, dignity, and social standing for

three minutes of glory on a tiny stage? If so, you're ready for a Karaoke Date.

If, on the other hand, you answered no to those questions, you're even more ready for a Karaoke Date. Shedding your inhibitions with your honey—being willing to risk looking foolish *together*—can be a great bonding experience.

MAKE IT HAPPEN

With a little preparation and the right spirit, you can make your Karaoke Date one to remember. Here are a few suggestions to keep in mind.

1 *Organize a Karaoke Night yourself, if possible.*
Many churches have karaoke machines for their youth groups and young adult groups. Check with your church staff to see if you could use the machine for an evening with your church friends. That way, you'll avoid the hassles of the bar scene.

If your church doesn't have a machine, one of your friends or neighbors might. If so, organize a karaoke-themed block party.

2 *Find the right atmosphere.*
Not all karaoke joints are created equal. If possible, scout some locations ahead of time. Find the one where you and your significant other would feel most comfortable.

3 *Be your date's biggest fan.*
This is especially important if your date is an introvert or uncomfortable getting up in front of a crowd. Encourage others to join you in cheering him or her on. Make him or her feel supported and appreciated.

4 *Just duet.*
Do not pass up an opportunity to sing at least one song together—the cheesier, the better. If you have friends who will preserve the performance (in video or in pictures) with their phones, make sure you get a copy. (You can decide whether to post it online or not.)

FINISH STRONG

Before you end your Karaoke Date, talk with each other about the experience. Use the following questions as needed to guide your discussion.

- ▶ On a scale of 1 to 10, how embarrassing was that for you? Explain.

- ▶ Did the fact that I was here make you more or less self-conscious? Explain.

- ▶ In what areas can we be more transparent and fearless with each other—and less self-conscious?

 ## MIND YOUR LANGUAGE

If your date's primary love language is Receiving Gifts, surprise him or her with a trophy to commemorate your Karaoke Date. If possible, have the engraving refer specifically to their performance. For example, it might say, "Best Rendition of 'Piano Man'" or "Best Attempt at a High Note." A trophy with a great inside joke between the two of you would make a unique and thoughtful gift.

TAKE IT TO GOD

Before your date, spend some time in prayer as a couple. Thank God for giving you someone you can have fun with—someone who will love you no matter what. Ask the Lord to

- ▶ bless the time you spend with each other;
- ▶ help you maintain a game spirit throughout your Karaoke Date;
- ▶ help you offer encouragement and support to each other.

DIG DEEP

Want to check out some more passages that talk about the importance of enjoying life? Try these.

- ▶ Proverbs 17:22
- ▶ Ecclesiastes 2:24
- ▶ Ecclesiastes 3:1–8
- ▶ Ecclesiastes 3:13

- ▶ John 16:24
- ▶ Devotional reading from *The Love Languages Devotional Bible*, page 642

TO NEXT DATE

THE JIGSAW PUZZLE DATE

WORDS TO GROW ON

How great is our Lord! His power is absolute!
His understanding is beyond comprehension!

PSALM 147:5

Quality time does not mean we must spend
our moments gazing into each other's eyes.
It may mean doing something together that we
both enjoy. The particular activity is secondary,
only a means to creating the sense of togetherness.
The important thing is not the activity itself but
the emotions that are created between both.

GARY CHAPMAN

21

SET THE SCENE

The words *Jigsaw Puzzle Date* by themselves may not
conjure up visions of romance and excitement. But
when you add words like "next to a warm fireplace"
or "with your favorite romantic music playing in the
background," the possibilities become a little clearer.

Piecing together a jigsaw puzzle lends itself both to engaging conversations and comfortable silences. If you come prepared with a few discussion-starter ideas, you may be surprised where your conversation takes you.

MAKE IT HAPPEN

The more effort you put into your Jigsaw Puzzle Date, the more you and your significant other will get out of it. Here are a few tips to consider.

1 *Create a great atmosphere.*
Whether it's a snowy evening by the fire or a summer weekend afternoon, try to set the mood by having your favorite romantic music playing in the background. Plan some yummy snacks to help put your date over the top.

2 *Learn from each other as you work together.*
Do you have differing methods for working puzzles? If so, talk about them. Does your puzzle-working style reveal something about you—say, that you have a strong preference for organization and orderliness? Talk about that, too. See how much you can learn about each other before the puzzle is done.

3 *Be prepared to keep the conversation flowing.*
Before the date, brainstorm a few topics or questions you can use as needed to guide your conversation. For example, you might ask, "Was there ever a time when you felt that your life was in pieces—and that you couldn't see the big picture to put things back together again?" Be prepared with your own example to break the ice. That might encourage your significant other to share more freely.

If you need to use note cards as prompts, don't be embarrassed. Your date will be flattered that you put such effort into the evening.

4 *Don't let the puzzle get in the way of a good evening.* There's no dating law that says you *have* to finish the puzzle. If the conversation gets good, or if you're married and the romantic fireside setting gets the best of you both, don't hesitate to abandon the puzzle.

FINISH STRONG

Before you end your Jigsaw Puzzle Date, spend a few minutes talking about the experience. Use the following questions as needed to guide your discussion.

▶ What are some of the "puzzle pieces" each of us brought to our relationship? ("Puzzle pieces" may include skills, expectations, needs, and various forms of personal baggage.)

▶ What's been the biggest challenge in making those pieces fit together?

▶ How does it make you feel to know that God sees the completed picture of our relationship and knows exactly how our pieces fit together?

MIND YOUR LANGUAGE

If your date's primary love language is Receiving Gifts, create a customized puzzle—using their favorite picture of the two of you—for your date. (A quick Internet search using the keywords "create your own jigsaw puzzle" should give you all the information you need.)

After you complete the puzzle, glue the pieces together and find a suitable frame for the picture. Your significant other will have a memento of your Jigsaw Puzzle Date to display.

TAKE IT TO GOD

Before your Jigsaw Puzzle Date, spend some time in prayer together. Married couples can thank God for combining the individual pieces of your two lives and joining them together to create a unified whole. Ask Him to help you

- ► come up with some memorably effective discussion starters;

- ► guide your conversation so you'll be able to learn more about each other;

- ► work as a team toward a common goal: completing the puzzle.

DIG DEEP

Want to check out some more passages that talk about God's ability to see the "big picture"? Try these.

- ► 1 Samuel 2:3
- ► Job 28:24
- ► Job 37:16
- ► Isaiah 55:9
- ► 1 John 3:19–20

- ► Devotional reading from *The Love Languages Devotional Bible*, page 987

THE ICE-SKATING DATE

WORDS TO GROW ON

Two people are better off than one, for they can help each other succeed. If one person falls, the other can reach out and help. But someone who falls alone is in real trouble.

ECCLESIASTES 4:9–10

Most people want to have a loving, supportive, understanding spouse. I'm convinced the fastest way to have such a spouse is to become a loving, supportive, understanding spouse.

GARY CHAPMAN

22

SET THE SCENE

The Ice-Skating Date is an embodiment of the truth of Ecclesiastes 4:9–10: "If one person falls, the other can reach out and help. But someone who falls alone is in real trouble." The less experience you have on skates, the more that truth becomes apparent.

Throughout the date, you should find yourselves literally supporting each other—for balance, steadiness, and security. Isn't that an awesome illustration of the kind of relationship God desires for us?

By itself, the Ice-Skating Date can be a fun, exhilarating experience. When paired with a seasonal activity—say, doing some Christmas window-shopping or checking out holiday lights and decorations—it can be truly memorable.

MAKE IT HAPPEN

If you both have experience on the frozen blades, you know what a great date ice-skating can be. If, however, you and your date are first-timers, here are a few tips to help you better prepare:

1 *Dress appropriately.*
Don't let temperature issues spoil your date. The rink, of course, will be necessarily cold. But the physical exertion of skating will get your blood pumping and heat your core; so make sure to dress in layers. (Speaking of layers, an extra layer or two of padding for your posterior may not be a bad idea.)

2 *Be prepared to laugh.*
If you're a rink rookie, you're going to fall. Awkwardly. Embarrassingly. And often. Sometimes you'll take each other down. Sometimes you'll take down complete strangers—maybe even innocent children.

The more easily you can laugh at yourself when those embarrassing falls occur, the more fun you're going to have.

3 *Save some energy for post-skating activities.*
The most popular time of year for ice-skating is the holiday season. Make plans to do something holiday related after your skating adventure, such as window-shopping or admiring the decorations and enjoying the holiday atmosphere.

FINISH STRONG

Before you end your Ice-Skating Date, spend a few minutes talking with each other about the experience. Use the following questions as needed to guide your discussion.

- ▶ Why does God put such emphasis on spouses supporting each other?

- ▶ In what areas of daily life do we support each other?

- ▶ In what areas do we need to offer each other more support?

MIND YOUR LANGUAGE

If you're married and your spouse's primary love language is Physical Touch, this is the perfect date. Ice-skating is a tactile bonanza. In fact, if you're rookie skaters, you'll find it hard *not* to touch each other with all of the falling and getting up you'll be doing.

In this case, though, we're talking about *purposeful* contact —say, a reassuring arm around the waist to steady your spouse or a quick hug and kiss on the ground after you've both wiped out. At the very least, you can spend most of your time holding hands.

TAKE IT TO GOD

Before your date, spend some time in prayer as a couple. Thank God that you've discovered the truth of Ecclesiastes 4:9–10—that you have each other to lean on. Ask Him to

- ▶ bless your time together during your Ice-Skating Date;
- ▶ keep you safe on the ice—and keep others safe from you;
- ▶ help you come away with a deeper appreciation for the support your significant other offers you.

DIG DEEP

Want to check out some more passages that talk about the importance of supporting and encouraging each other? Try these.

- ▶ Matthew 25:35–40
- ▶ Romans 12:10
- ▶ Ephesians 5:22–33
- ▶ 1 Thessalonians 5:11

- ▶ Hebrews 10:25
- ▶ Devotional reading from *The Love Languages Devotional Bible*, page 1242

TO NEXT DATE

THE ARCADE DATE

WORDS TO GROW ON

*Then he said, "I tell you the truth,
unless you turn from your sins and
become like little children, you will never
get into the Kingdom of Heaven."*

MATTHEW 18:3

Enjoy today what you have today.

GARY CHAPMAN

23

SET THE SCENE

Jesus encourages His followers to bring a childlike
perspective to our faith. Children are trusting, humble,
dependent, and able to be shaped and molded. Those
are the qualities Jesus wants in us. Those are the
qualities of difference makers for him.

We can all benefit from being more childlike
occasionally—not just for our spiritual health, but
for our emotional and relational health as well.

Children have the ability to set aside their cares and worries temporarily in order to pursue fun. That's what you're going to do on this date. The Arcade Date is designed to help you have fun with your inner child.

MAKE IT HAPPEN

How long has it been since you were in an arcade? You may be in for a bit of future shock, especially if you're not a gamer. With a little reconnaissance work, though, you may be able to find an arcade in your area that features some old-school games.

That would be ideal, because reconnecting with your youth is what this date is all about. If you're able to find some of your favorite games from childhood, test your skills again. Surrender to nostalgia. Help each other understand why those games meant something to you. Share a few of your arcade stories. Talk about the friends you used to play with. If your date has similar stories to tell, be an active listener.

Of course, if you see some cool-looking *new* games, feel free to indulge. Play as a team or against each other. Just make sure both of you get equal screen time. The Arcade Date will get boring very quickly if only one of you is playing.

The one childlike quality you'll want to avoid is hypercompetitiveness. If winning or doing well on a game becomes your focus, it's time for a priority check. Having fun with your date is Job #1.

Bringing along some of each other's favorite candies from childhood would be a nice touch!

FINISH STRONG

Before you end your Arcade Date, spend a few minutes talking with each other about the experience. Use the following questions as needed to guide your discussion.

- ▶ What does it mean to have a childlike faith?

- ▶ What are some of the things that happen to people's faith as they get older that Jesus wants us to avoid?

- ▶ How can we encourage each other to maintain a childlike faith?

MIND YOUR LANGUAGE

If your date's primary love language is Receiving Gifts, you'll want to find an arcade with a prize-redemption counter. This is how it works: as you play games, you earn tickets that you can redeem for prizes; the more tickets you earn, the bigger and better prizes you can get.

At the beginning of your Arcade Date, swing by the redemption counter. Look at all the prizes available, and have your sweetheart pick the one she'd like to take home. Your goal, then, is to earn enough tickets to get that prize.

TAKE IT TO GOD

Before your date, spend some time in prayer as a couple. Thank God for the good memories you have of your childhood. Thank Him for the lessons you learned that helped shape you and for the people who made a difference in your life. Ask Him to help you

- maintain a childlike enthusiasm for your Arcade Date;

- open up to each other about your childhood memories and experiences;

- identify specific ways you can be more childlike in your faith.

DIG DEEP

Want to check out some more passages that talk about the importance of a childlike perspective? Try these.

- Psalm 8:2

- Matthew 19:14

- Matthew 21:15–16

- Mark 10:13–16

- Luke 18:17

- Devotional reading from *The Love Languages Devotional Bible*, page 520

THE CANDLELIGHT DATE

24

WORDS TO GROW ON

*There are three things that amaze me—
no, four things that I don't understand:
how an eagle glides through the sky, how a
snake slithers on a rock, how a ship navigates
the ocean, how a man loves a woman.*

PROVERBS 30:18–19

*Because it is God's best for you, the journey
toward intimacy is well worth the commitment.*

GARY CHAPMAN

SET THE SCENE

Romance comes easily to couples in the early stages
of a relationship. They think nothing of professing
their love in the purplest of prose or planning
elaborate gestures to convey their feelings.

As relationships mature, however, the business
of planning a life together takes center stage.

Romance often becomes a relic of the past—a luxury for people with more time on their hands and fewer things competing for their attention. Romance ends up a casualty of "real-life practicalities."

The Candlelight Date offers you a chance to reclaim romance in your relationship. The candlelight itself is key, because it physically and symbolically illuminates only the two of you; everything else is left in darkness for the duration of your date.

MAKE IT HAPPEN

Candlelight is an absolute essential for this date. Its symbolic and mood-setting elements are key. Beyond that, though, everything is negotiable. What do you want to do during your Candlelight Date?

Eating dinner is an obvious option—but not just any dinner will do. Think romance. What are the most romantic meal ideas you can come up with—or find online? You can embrace romantic clichés, or you can transcend them. Either way, you'll need to do careful advance planning to make sure you have every base covered.

Beyond the meal, you'll need to consider your attire for the date—and then pull out all the stops. The sport jacket and tie that she said you looked so handsome in? Put 'em on. The dress that makes you feel self-conscious but makes his eyes pop out? Perfect for this occasion.

Your topics of conversation should continue the romantic vibe. If you're married or engaged, share about the first time you realized your spouse was "the one." Talk about your honeymoon. At some point during your date, talk about the candlelight. If the light represents Christ, how can you make sure you stay close to it, as individuals and as a couple? What happens if you get too far away from it? How can you figuratively take that light with you wherever you go?

FINISH STRONG

After your Candlelight Date, spend a little time talking about the experience. Use the following questions as needed to guide your discussion.

- ▶ What are some specific things we can do to keep romance alive in our relationship—even in the grind of everyday life?

- ▶ What are some specific things we can do to keep Christ's light at the center of our relationship?

- ▶ What are some specific things we can do to take the light to others?

MIND YOUR LANGUAGE

If your date's primary love language is Words of Affirmation, you can send the romance level of your date through the roof with a carefully worded greeting card. If you find one that says absolutely everything you want to say to your significant other, get it. If not, buy a blank card and write your own romantic message.

Don't be shy. Don't be self-conscious. Tell your date what you love about them and how they make you feel—something that will make your date smile. Send a message your loved one will go over and over again, whenever they need a pick-me-up.

TAKE IT TO GOD

Before your date, spend some time in prayer as a couple. Thank God for the arc of your relationship—how He has allowed it to deepen over time. Thank Him that you're able to share romance and intimacy with each other. Ask God to help you

- ▸ set and maintain the proper mood for your Candlelight Date;
- ▸ eliminate distractions for the duration of your date;
- ▸ find the right words to express yourself to each other in a meaningful way.

DIG DEEP

Here are some additional passages you can use for your Candlelight Date.

- ▸ Proverbs 5:19
- ▸ Song of Songs 1:2
- ▸ Song of Songs 4:10
- ▸ Song of Songs 8:7

- ▸ Ephesians 5:25
- ▸ Devotional reading from *The Love Languages Devotional Bible*, page 646

TO NEXT DATE

THE GARDENING DATE

WORDS TO GROW ON

I am my lover's, and my lover is mine.
He browses among the lilies.

SONG OF SONGS 6:3

We need to nurture, allow time for change,
and then trust God to do the work of the
Master Gardener.

GARY CHAPMAN

25

SET THE SCENE

Looking for an inexpensive date that will create
time with your significant other in an outdoor
setting? One that gives you a chance to break a
sweat—and, if you are married, may increase your
house's curb appeal? If so, you may be in the market
for a Gardening Date. After all, not all dates have
to involve going out. With a little creativity, you
and your significant other can have an excellent

time together working in your garden—or your yard (or your parent's yard). If you don't have a yard, consider a specific project in a parent's yard or in the yard of someone you know.

The Gardening Date lends itself to some quality conversation—not just about plants and flowers, but about the things that are "growing" in your relationship, the "weeds" that need to be tended to, and so forth. You don't have to force the analogy, but you can use it as a discussion starter.

MAKE IT HAPPEN

Before your Gardening Date, it might be a good idea to sit down with each other and talk about some of the things that could be done in your garden and yard. Make a list, if necessary—just so the two of you are on the same page regarding what you'll be doing. Remember to choose tasks the two of you can do together, or at least in the same vicinity.

Make sure you don't lose sight of your priorities. This isn't a workday, per se; it's a date. If you want to take a break over a glass of iced tea and relaxed conversation, or spend some quiet time lazily staring at the sky, go for it! If you feel like starting a water fight while you're hosing down your garden tools, set your nozzle for "fun." Let's put it this way: if you're concerned about not getting enough work done during your Gardening Date, you're missing the point of the activity.

If your gardening chores require a trip to the store, stop off for some coffee or ice cream on the way home. After you've finished your work and cleaned up, treat yourselves to dinner at your favorite restaurant. In other words, don't pass up an opportunity to steal some nonworking time with each other.

FINISH STRONG

Before you end your Gardening Date, spend a few minutes talking about the experience. Use the following questions as needed to guide your discussion.

- ► What are some of the things we've "grown" in our relationship?

- ► What are some of the "weeds" we've had to clear out along the way?

- ► What can we do to make our relationship even more productive?

MIND YOUR LANGUAGE

If your date's primary love language is Acts of Service, tackle a garden or yardwork chore that's needed to be done for a long time. You might plant a tree, spread some mulch, or weed a flowerbed.

If you're feeling especially ambitious, you might ask your significant other to make a wish list of the top three chores he or she would like to have done—and then proceed to tackle them as part of your Gardening Date. If you manage to complete them, maintaining a positive attitude all the while, your date's love tank will be overflowing by the end of your date.

TAKE IT TO GOD

Before your date, spend some time in prayer as a couple. Praise God for the marvels of His creation—the way a small seed can bloom into something incredible. Thank Him for nurturing your relationship with your date and helping it to grow. Ask Him to

- ▶ bless the time you spend together;
- ▶ help you examine your relationship from His perspective;
- ▶ identify specific ways you can make your relationship more productive.

DIG DEEP

If you're looking for more passages that talk about gardening, try these.

- ▶ Isaiah 5:7
- ▶ Jeremiah 29:5
- ▶ Amos 9:14
- ▶ Matthew 13:32

- ▶ Luke 13:19
- ▶ Devotional reading from *The Love Languages Devotional Bible*, page 1102

THE CULINARY DATE

WORDS TO GROW ON

*A bowl of vegetables with someone you love
is better than steak with someone you hate.*

PROVERBS 15:17

26

*Divorce is the result of a lack of preparation
for marriage and the failure to learn the skills
of working together as teammates in an
intimate relationship.*

GARY CHAPMAN

SET THE SCENE

If you are both foodies, you likely won't need
much prompting to give the Culinary Date a shot.
If, however, one of you is a stranger to the kitchen,
you may be a little reluctant. In that case, whoever
is more experienced may need to serve as a mentor
of sorts to the other. As long as that mentoring
is given and received with a good attitude, you
shouldn't have a problem.

You'll find that cooking together involves no small amount of cooperation and teamwork. The Culinary Date should give you a pretty good idea of how well the two of you work together.

MAKE IT HAPPEN

You can take your Culinary Date in one of a couple different directions. The first option is to prepare and enjoy a meal together. Obviously, the meal should require a little more effort than opening a jar of tomato sauce and a box of angel hair pasta. Beyond that, though, you can decide how complicated or time intensive you want your meal preparation to be.

After you've decided on a menu lineup—appetizers, main dish, side dishes, and dessert—come up with a plan of attack. Here are a few things to keep in mind.

1 *Do the shopping together.*
There will be no solo ventures where this meal is concerned. Every step along the way should be taken together. That means a joint trip to the grocery store to get everything you'll need.

2 *Work as a team until the job is done.*
This is not a place for the more kitchen-savvy of the two of you to do all the substantial work while the other person is relegated to table-setting duty. Both of you should be equally responsible for the meal's success. That may require more than a dollop of patience and cooperation, but since when are those bad things?

3 *Do the cleanup work together.*
Remember, the date doesn't end when the food is consumed. Cleanup time is a great time for conversation. For example,

you might talk about how your relationship—and, if you're married, your household—would be affected if you started doing more daily tasks together.

Your second option is to enroll in a one-day cooking class together. You can find information online regarding classes that are offered in your area. Once you know your options, you can choose a class that looks interesting to both of you.

FINISH STRONG

Before you end your Culinary Date, talk about the experience as a couple. Use the following questions as needed to guide your discussion.

- ▶ What qualities did God see in us when He decided that we would make a good team?

- ▶ What are some of the challenges we face when it comes to working together?

- ▶ How could we put our teamwork to use in a volunteer ministry setting?

MIND YOUR LANGUAGE

If your date's primary love language is Acts of Service, you can make a huge impression by preparing one special item just for your date. Choose one of your date's favorite dishes and locate the recipe. If it's a childhood favorite, you might check with his or her family to find the recipe. Don't change plans to cook the rest of the meal together, but consider preparing this dish ahead of time and bringing it out just before you sit down to eat your special meal.

TAKE IT TO GOD

Before your Culinary Date, spend some time in prayer together. Thank God for the abundance of His blessings. Thank Him for supplying your needs every day. Ask Him to

- help you maintain a spirit of gratitude for what you've been given and what you have access to;

- bless and watch over those who don't know where their next meal is coming from;

- bless your efforts to work as a team—during the Culinary Date and beyond.

DIG DEEP

Here are a few more Bible passages that fit the food and team-work themes of the Culinary Date.

- Psalm 104:14–15
- Proverbs 27:17
- Ecclesiastes 4:9–12
- Isaiah 1:19

- 1 Corinthians 12:20–25
- Devotional reading from *The Love Languages Devotional Bible*, page 723

TO NEXT DATE

THE APPLE–PICKING DATE

WORDS TO GROW ON

*Let each generation tell its children of
your mighty acts; let them proclaim your power.*

PSALM 145:4

*Taking advice requires humility
and shows wisdom.*

GARY CHAPMAN

27

SET THE SCENE

Apple-picking is a fine activity, but the *real* purpose
of this date is to spend time with a couple who've
been married for years—marriage mentors, if you
will. If picking apples is something you'd all enjoy,
head for your local orchard. If not, choose a different
activity. As long as the four of you are able to spend
time together in a relaxed setting, talking and
getting to know each other, it doesn't really matter
what you do.

Spending the day with the right couple can have a remarkable effect on your relationship. You may discover that the quirks of your relationship are not quite as unique as you thought—or that the problems that seem insurmountable now can, in fact, be overcome. The ideal mentoring couple will help you learn from their successes as well as their failures.

MAKE IT HAPPEN

If apple-picking is what you choose to do, you'll need to find the closest orchard and get all the information you need to plan your date. And then you'll need to focus on the important stuff.

1 *Find the right mentors.*
This is the key to the whole endeavor. The right mentors could make a real difference in your lives. The wrong ones could make for a very long day at the orchard. Choose wisely—and with a lot of prayer.

The obvious place to start your search is at church. You're looking for a spiritually mature couple who have been married much longer than you have. They may not necessarily view themselves as mentors, but they have enough life experience to have amassed some wisdom along the way. If their personalities mesh with yours, all the better.

If you know such a couple, approach them with the idea of an "Apple-Picking Date" (or whatever you choose to do)—that is, an opportunity for you to pick their brains and be mentored by them regarding marriage and family. If you don't know of such a couple, ask your pastor or a church leader for input.

2 *Brainstorm some questions ahead of time.*
You don't want things to get awkward—or to be at a loss for conversation. So come up with a list of topics and issues that you'd like to get some input on. You might want to share your list with the mentoring couple before the date so they have a chance to prepare.

3 *Keep things light.*
Remember, it's a date, not a counseling session. Laugh. Have fun. Learn while you enjoy yourselves.

FINISH STRONG

Before you end your Apple-Picking Date, spend a few minutes talking to your spouse about the experience—and what you'll take away from it. Use the following questions as needed to guide your discussion.

- ▶ Why is it important for us to learn from other people's God-given wisdom?

- ▶ What's the most important lesson we'll take away from this date?

- ▶ How can we serve as mentors to others?

MIND YOUR LANGUAGE

If your date's primary language is Words of Affirmation, be sure to talk your date up every opportunity you get during your Apple-Picking Date. Share some of the qualities and gifts your date brings to your relationship. Talk about what you've learned from him or her and how it's influenced your life.

Without overdoing it, you want to make sure your loved one comes away from your Apple-Picking Date feeling affirmed and loved.

TAKE IT TO GOD

Before your date, spend some time in prayer with each other. Thank God for the plan in His Word that calls for one generation to mentor the next. Thank Him for the people who have served as mentors in your lives. Ask Him to

▶ lead you to a couple who are willing and able to serve as mentors;

▶ bless your time together on your Apple-Picking Date;

▶ help you influence the lives of your mentors as much as they are influencing yours.

DIG DEEP

Want to check out some more passages that talk about the importance of mentoring? Try these.

▶ Psalm 71:18

▶ Proverbs 27:17

▶ 2 Timothy 2:2

▶ Titus 2:3–5

▶ 1 Peter 5:1–5

▶ Devotional reading from *The Love Languages Devotional Bible*, page 376

TO NEXT DATE

THE ROMANTIC MOVIE DATE

28

WORDS TO GROW ON

*Kiss me and kiss me again, for your love
is sweeter than wine.*

SONG OF SONGS 1:2

*Covenant love is conscious love.
It is intentional love. It is commitment to love
no matter what. It requires thought and action.
It does not wait for the encouragement of
warm emotions but chooses to look out for
the interest of the other party because
you are committed to the other's well-being.*

GARY CHAPMAN

SET THE SCENE

Many popular expressions of love and romance can
be traced back to Hollywood. The right actors with
the right script can cast a powerful romantic spell on
audiences. Chances are, you're conjuring up images
of your favorite screen romances while you read this.

For this date, you're going to embrace the clichés and improbabilities of Hollywood romance and watch a romantic movie with your significant other.

MAKE IT HAPPEN

The easiest thing to do would be to choose an old standby—a favorite romantic movie that you and/or your date have already seen a half dozen times or more. Resist this urge. Instead, look for a movie neither of you has seen.

A quick online search for "best romantic movies" will yield dozens of possibilities. Here are eight to get you started. Some of the titles may be familiar to you already. Every one is romantic enough to meet the criteria of your date.

▶ *Gone with the Wind (1939)*
 If you prefer a romance set against the backdrop of the Civil War, this is the one for you.

▶ *Casablanca (1942)*
 If your quest is to find the greatest romantic movie ever made, start here.

▶ *An Affair to Remember (1957)*
 If you're in the mood for a tearjerker, grab some tissues and watch this one.

- *West Side Story (1961)*

  If you prefer romance among the singing and dancing street gangs of New York, try this classic musical.

- *The Princess Bride (1987)*

  If you prefer laughs with your screen romance, this film will do nicely.

- *Beauty and the Beast (1991)*

  If you love animated romance, be prepared to sing along while you watch this Disney classic.

- *Sense and Sensibility (1995)*

  If you prefer nineteenth-century romance, check out the film version of this literary classic.

- *Titanic (1997)*

  If you prefer romance tinged with tragedy, why not try one of the highest-grossing movies of all time?

Afterward, talk about the movie—your favorite scenes, favorite characters, and favorite lines. Compare it to other romantic movies you've watched together. Talk briefly about the parts of a relationship that romantic movies almost never show: the boring and mundane stuff, the petty bickering, the challenge of keeping romance alive in the daily grind of life.

FINISH STRONG

Before you end your Romantic Movie Date, spend a few minutes talking as a couple about the experience. Use the following questions as needed to guide your discussion.

- What parts of our relationship would make an interesting romantic movie?

- If the movie were a true-to-life biographical film, can we see how God's purposes in our relationship would figure into the plot?

- What is God's will for our relationship?

MIND YOUR LANGUAGE

If you're married and your spouse's primary language is Physical Touch, create a "cocoon" for the two of you to share while you watch the movie. Wrap yourselves together in blankets and surround yourselves with pillows. Get cozy and enjoy a couple of hours of prolonged physical contact. For added emphasis, give your spouse little squeezes during romantic scenes as a way of saying, "That reminds me of us."

TAKE IT TO GOD

Before your date, spend some time in prayer with each other. Thank God for His gift of creativity—and the fact that we can find enjoyment or enlightenment from the creative works of others. Ask the Lord to

- bless your time together;

- give you a perspective on love and romance that's deeper and longer lasting than that portrayed in movies;

- help you express your appreciation to each other for creating a romance that's better than anything Hollywood could come up with.

DIG DEEP

Want to check out some more passages that talk about love?
Try these.

- ▶ Proverbs 10:12
- ▶ Song of Songs 2:2–3
- ▶ Song of Songs 3:4
- ▶ 1 Peter 4:8

- ▶ 1 John 3:18
- ▶ Devotional reading from
  *The Love Languages
  Devotional Bible*, page 1320

THE HIKING DATE

WORDS TO GROW ON

Trust in the Lord with all your heart;
do not depend on your own understanding.
Seek his will in all you do, and he will
show you which path to take.

PROVERBS 3:5–6

Scripture calls us to live righteously by
choosing the right path, and obeying the
rules of God, because we believe they are
designed for our well being. When we walk in
righteousness, we experience peace.

GARY CHAPMAN

SET THE SCENE

Like many other dates in this book, the Hiking
Date can have bigger implications than its title
or description indicates. On one level, you can
enjoy some time together in an outdoor setting.

You can admire the scenery. You can get a good workout. You can explore places you've never been before.

On another level, you can use the elements of this date as a jumping-off point for an interesting discussion about your relationship—one that perhaps will open a discussion of future hopes and dreams, or even shift the direction of your relationship.

MAKE IT HAPPEN

Planning your Hiking Date should be easy. Here are a few tips to get you started and on your way.

1 *Choose a good spot.*
Make sure the area you choose allows hikers. Getting arrested for trespassing would put a serious crimp in your hiking plans! Make sure the trail and terrain are suitable for you and your significant other's skill, health, and activity levels.

2 *Think in terms of destination.*
Is there a place either of you has wanted to see? Is there a mountain you want to climb or a park or lake you want to visit? If so, plan your hike with that destination in mind.

3 *Watch the forecast.*
If the weather looks iffy, make sure you have a backup plan. Don't try to press on in unfavorable conditions.

4 *Pack well.*
Each of you will need hiking shoes, two pairs of thick socks, a hat, weather-appropriate clothing, a flashlight, a full water bottle or two, a compass, a map of the area, first-aid supplies, plenty of food, and a sturdy backpack to hold it all.

5   *Leave a trail of figurative breadcrumbs.*
Make sure more than one person (not including your
date!) knows

- where you'll be hiking;

- what direction you'll be heading;

- what time you expect to return.

If something were to happen, it's good to know that people
know where to look for you.

FINISH STRONG

Before you end your Hiking Date, spend a few minutes talking
with each other about the experience. Use the following
questions as needed to guide your discussion.

- In hiking terms, what has our journey as a couple
  been like?

- Where have we gotten lost—or at least momentarily
  turned around—along the way?

- Where do you think God's path will ultimately lead us?

MIND YOUR LANGUAGE

If your date's primary love language is Acts of
Service, you can fill his tank by preparing his
backpack for him. The more "personal" touches
you include in your Act of Service, the more meaningful your
gesture will be. For example, don't just pack *any* water bottle;
pack his *favorite* water bottle—the one with the logo of his
beloved team on it or the one that came in the gift bag when

he ran the half-marathon. When it comes to packing food, make sure some of her favorite snacks are represented.

TAKE IT TO GOD

Before your date, spend some time in prayer as a couple. Thank God for the beauty of His creation—and for the opportunity to enjoy it during your Hiking Date. Ask Him to

- ▶ protect you during your hike and keep you safe from harm;

- ▶ open your eyes to aspects of His creation that you've never noticed before;

- ▶ guide your discussion with each other in a way that you both come away from the date with a deeper appreciation of nature—and a deeper appreciation of your life journey together.

DIG DEEP

You can find dozens of Bible passages that fit the theme of this date—verses that talk about walking with the Lord, keeping your paths straight, enjoying God's creation, and more. Here are a few to get you started.

- ▶ Deuteronomy 5:33
- ▶ Psalm 119:105
- ▶ Psalm 119:133
- ▶ 2 Corinthians 5:7
- ▶ Ephesians 2:10

- ▶ Devotional reading from *The Love Languages Devotional Bible*, page 769

TO NEXT DATE

THE PARK BENCH DATE

WORDS TO GROW ON

All Scripture is inspired by God and is useful to teach us what is true and to make us realize what is wrong in our lives. It corrects us when we are wrong and teaches us to do what is right.

2 TIMOTHY 3:16

All of us are more likely to communicate our inner thoughts and feelings if we believe that someone genuinely wants to hear what we want to say and will not condemn us.

GARY CHAPMAN

SET THE SCENE

The Park Bench Date involves sitting on a park bench with each other, and reading a favorite book, article, letters, Bible passages, or more to each other.

Don't be fooled, though. This idea isn't nearly as sedate as it seems! Granted, it doesn't involve much movement or action. But it does involve an exchange of ideas—a revealing of self. The idea here is not just to read random books and articles to each other. It's to share passages that have deeply affected you—words that have helped shape you and make you into the person you are today.

MAKE IT HAPPEN

The Park Bench Date is a date that calls for your *best* preparation.

If you're willing to do the work, this date—this one afternoon spent on a park bench—could be something you remember for the rest of your lives. Here's what you need to do:

1 *Spend some time compiling your sources.*
Think about the books, articles, stories, Bible verses, song lyrics, and other passages that have influenced your life. Start with your favorite authors, and make a list of the titles that you immediately remember that influenced you. Bring a variety of material—especially works that changed how you looked at the world—or even how you looked at God and His Word. Use bookmarks and sticky notes to mark passages you want to share.

2 *Crack open a journal or two.*
Don't limit yourself to the written works of others. Share your own words as well. If you keep a journal, bring one along and find passages that reflect different sides of you.

3 *Find the right setting.*
If finding a park bench is not convenient, try someplace else. You may choose to sit on a blanket on the beach, or find a nice place with a beautiful view. Just make sure the spot you choose is quiet and private.

4

Be the best listener ever.
Reward each one's willingness to open up to the other.
Listen attentively to the passages your date shares, and ask questions that encourage them to tell you more.

FINISH STRONG

Before you end your Park Bench Date, spend a few minutes talking about the experience. Use the following questions as needed to guide your discussion.

▶ What are the most surprising things we learned about each other today?

▶ If someone had overheard us sharing our passages, what conclusions might they have drawn?

▶ What Bible passage should we adopt as "ours"—the one that best sums up our relationship or our outlook on life?

 ## MIND YOUR LANGUAGE

If your significant other's primary love language is Quality Time, choose one of the books they share with you during your Park Bench Date— preferably something they identify as one of their favorites— and suggest that the two of you read and discuss it together.

Set aside time frequently and regularly to devote to the book. Take notes. When you're finished with a chapter, discuss it together. Let your special someone know that what's important to him or her is important to you.

TAKE IT TO GOD

Before your date, spend some time in prayer with each other. Thank God for the many different ways in which He teaches, inspires, and motivates us. Ask God to

- ▶ bless your time together;
- ▶ help you come up with a variety of fun and interesting sources that will give your date insight into what makes you tick;
- ▶ give you the words to share your own sources and to ask illuminating questions about what your significant other shares.

DIG DEEP

Not surprisingly, the Bible has a lot to say about the power of the written word. Here are a few passages you may want to consult before (or after) your date.

- ▶ Joshua 1:8
- ▶ Psalm 119:105; also vv. 89–93
- ▶ Matthew 4:4
- ▶ Hebrews 4:12
- ▶ Devotional reading from *The Love Languages Devotional Bible*, page 1301

TO NEXT DATE

THE DANCING DATE

31

WORDS TO GROW ON

A time to cry and a time to laugh.
A time to grieve and a time to dance.

ECCLESIASTES 3:4

We are relational creatures.
All humans live in community, and
most people seek social interaction.

GARY CHAPMAN

SET THE SCENE

Of *course* you should take your significant other dancing! Dancing encompasses what a committed relationship is all about: two people working in rhythm together. Dancing is therapeutic. It allows you to forget about the deadlines, pressures, and problems of everyday life for a while. It also offers a great cardio workout.

Dancing is romantic. How can you spend an evening with each other—your arms wrapped around each other—without igniting the embers of romance?

MAKE IT HAPPEN

We can't make you a great dancer, but we can give you tips for planning a great Dancing Date. You'll need three things.

1 *The Right Venue*
The kind of dancing you choose to do will depend on both of your preference in music. If your tastes differ radically, you'll need to find a compromise that works for both of you. A little reconnaissance work before the date will go a long way toward ensuring a good time.

Find a club that feels comfortable to you—one that

- ▶ plays a mix of music you both enjoy;
- ▶ has a good vibe;
- ▶ caters to people your age;
- ▶ has an inviting dance floor.

2 *The Right Attire*
The Dancing Date allows (encourages) you to dress a little flashier than usual. Depending on the club you choose, you may need to meet certain dress standards in order to get in. If you have an opportunity to scout locations before your date, make sure you ask about dress codes.

Of course, you'll need to consider comfort, too—especially when it comes to shoes. One blister in the wrong place can end your evening prematurely. Whatever you wear, make sure it allows you to move around freely and without discomfort.

3 *The Right Attitude*
The fear of embarrassment should have no place in your Dancing Date! This is about spending an evening with your special someone in your arms, moving around to good music. Who cares if . . . your . . . rhythm . . . is a . . . little . . . off?

Don't be self-conscious about your moves. Just do the best you can and have fun. If you and your date are, shall we say, "unequally yoked" when it comes to dancing skills, make sure the more accomplished one stays patient and encouraging.

FINISH STRONG

Before you end your Dancing Date, spend a few minutes talking as a couple about the experience. Use the following questions as needed to guide your discussion.

▶ Why did David choose dancing as a means of worshiping God?

▶ How can self-consciousness interfere with our worship?

▶ How can we become more spontaneous and less self-conscious about our worship?

 ## MIND YOUR LANGUAGE

If your dancing skills are so rusty (nonexistent) that the idea of going to a club makes you break out in a cold sweat (and not in a funky, James Brown way), you may want to opt instead for some dance lessons.

This will be a special treat if your significant other's primary love language is Quality Time. Once a week you'll have a standing date to spend time together, learning new dances and perfecting your moves as a couple. Make sure you keep that time blocked out on your schedule so that nothing interferes with it.

TAKE IT TO GOD

Before your date, spend some time in prayer together. Thank God for His gift of music and dance. Thank Him for creating us as romantic beings—people who are drawn together by internal and external stimuli. Ask Him to help you

- overcome any shyness or self-consciousness that may get in the way of enjoying your Dancing Date;
- honor Him with the way you conduct yourselves on the dance floor;
- come away from your date with a renewed appreciation of—and passion for—each other.

DIG DEEP

The Bible makes several references to dancing with joyful abandon. Here's a sampling of verses you may want to check out.

- 2 Samuel 6:14
- Psalm 30:11
- Psalm 149:3
- Psalm 150:4
- Jeremiah 31:13

- Devotional reading from *The Love Languages Devotional Bible*, page 650

TO NEXT DATE

THE ZOO DATE

32

SET THE SCENE

Is there a better place for a casual, relaxed date
than your local zoo? Aside from the occasional
dolphin show, you're on no schedule. You don't
have to worry about getting to a certain place at
a certain time. You can move at your own pace.

A zoo setting also allows you to indulge in two worthwhile pastimes: admiring God's creation and talking. If you approach your day among the animals with a sense of wonder and awe, you'll come away with a renewed appreciation for the Creator. And if you spend a large portion of that time in casual-yet-meaningful conversation with your loved one, you'll come away with a renewed appreciation for each other.

MAKE IT HAPPEN

Chances are, you have both probably taken trips to the zoo since you were kids. You've seen it all. Lions and tigers and bears no longer provoke an "Oh, my!" reaction from you.

In order to make your Zoo Date stand out from all your other visits, you're going to need some memorable conversation starters. After all, few date venues lend themselves to talking more easily than a zoo.

Here are some discussion ideas that may come in handy during the long walk from the monkey house to the aquatic center.

- ► What are your favorite zoo memories from childhood? Did you love visiting or did you find it boring? Why?

- ► If you'd been given Adam's job of naming the animals, what would you have done differently? In your opinion, which names don't go with their corresponding animals? What would have been better names for them?

- ► What do you think life was like in the garden of Eden before the fall, with all of God's creatures living in harmony?

- What can we learn about God by looking at His handiwork in the animal world around us? (For example, an anteater's long snout and long tongue shows that God knows exactly what we need. A peacock's feathers show that God appreciates beauty. A penguin shows that God has a sense of humor.)

- What are our God-given responsibilities as caretakers of the natural world?

FINISH STRONG

Before you end your Zoo Date, spend a few minutes talking about the experience. Use the following questions as needed to guide your discussion.

- What's the most amazing aspect of God's creation?

- Why is it so easy to take God's creative work for granted?

- What specific steps can we take to maintain a proper sense of awe toward God's creation?

MIND YOUR LANGUAGE

If your date's primary love language is Quality Time, plan to spend plenty of it in the exhibit that houses his favorite animal. If you've never discussed his favorite animal before, this would be a great time to break the ice. Talk about why she has a fondness for a certain animal. Has it always been her favorite?

If you have time before your date, collect some information and trivia about your date's favorite animal and sprinkle it in your conversation.

TAKE IT TO GOD

Before your date, spend some time in prayer together. Praise God for the beauty of His creation, the heavens above and His creatures below. Cite as many examples of that beauty as you can think of. Thank Him for the opportunity to enjoy that beauty every day. Ask Him to

- ▶ bless the time you spend together on your Zoo Date;

- ▶ give you a renewed sense of appreciation, thankfulness, and awe for the variety of His creation;

- ▶ impress upon you your responsibilities as a caretaker of His creation.

DIG DEEP

The Bible makes it clear that God cares about every one of His creations. Here are just a few of the animal-related passages in His Word.

- ▶ Genesis 1:20–24
- ▶ Job 12:7–10
- ▶ Proverbs 12:10
- ▶ Matthew 6:26

- ▶ Luke 12:6
- ▶ Devotional reading from *The Love Languages Devotional Bible*, page 653

TO NEXT DATE

THE GARAGE SALE DATE

WORDS TO GROW ON

*Don't store up treasures here on earth,
where moths eat them and rust destroys them,
and where thieves break in and steal.*

MATTHEW 6:19

*When our trust is in God, we see money as an
instrument to be used for good under His direction.
Our greatest desires will be to please God as good
managers of the resources He has entrusted to us.*

GARY CHAPMAN

SET THE SCENE

On the surface, a garage sale is a practical event.
A chance for sellers to unclutter their lives, to
get rid of things that no longer have value to
them, and to make room for things that do. A
chance for buyers to find new treasures or fill
old needs. A chance to engage in transactions
that make everyone happy!

On a deeper level, a garage sale represents second chances
—an opportunity for repurposing or finding value and useful-
ness in a new setting. These are topics ripe for discussion—subjects that may hit close to home in your current circumstances.

For those reasons (and others), a garage sale is an ideal
setting for a date. You never know what treasures—real or
conversational—you may uncover.

MAKE IT HAPPEN

If you're serious about planning a Garage Sale Date, here are a
few tips you should consider.

1 *Decide on your role.*
Are you going to be buyers or sellers? If you choose to be
sellers, your date will require a lot more preparation—
rounding up your merchandise, setting up tables and racks,
putting price tags on everything . . . and so on. Make it fun by
reminiscing about some of the items you put up for sale.

If you choose to be buyers, you may want to make a list
of some things to look for at the garage sales you visit, as a
starting point.

2 *Check your calendar.*
In most areas, garage sales are seasonal activities. Certain
times of the year are hotbeds for garage sale activity. During
the first few weekends of summer, for example, garage sale
signs are inescapable. The more you know about the garage
sale schedule in your area, the better equipped you'll be to plan
your Garage Sale Date.

3 *Think beyond your own needs.*
What can you find at a garage sale that will benefit a homeless person in your area or victims of a natural disaster? Thinking in those terms may give new meaning and purpose to your Garage Sale Date.

FINISH STRONG

Before you end your Garage Sale Date, spend a few minutes talking about the experience. Use the following questions as needed to guide your discussion.

- ▶ What makes us want to hold on to "earthly treasures" for too long, whether money or other material things?

- ▶ What causes us to lose focus on our heavenly treasures?

- ▶ Who might benefit more than we do from some of our possessions?

MIND YOUR LANGUAGE

Chances are you have some boxes in the attic, in a crawlspace, or in storage that need to be purged—boxes containing items that need to be sorted as junk or keepsakes.

If your significant other's primary love language is Acts of Service, you could fill your date's love tank by setting aside a day to go through those boxes for him or her. Be thorough and purposeful in your sorting. The better the job you do, the more it will feel like love.

TAKE IT TO GOD

Before your date, spend some time in prayer together. Thank God for any financial and material possessions He's blessed you with. Praise Him for the fact that He supplies our needs—even when we're not sure what those needs are. Ask Him to

- ► bless your time together;
- ► give you financial wisdom during your date, whether you're buying or selling;
- ► guide your interactions with people so that He will be honored in each of them.

DIG DEEP

You can find several different Scripture passages that apply to the theme of this date. Here's a small sampling.

- ► Proverbs 2:4–5
- ► Matthew 6:20–21
- ► Matthew 19:21
- ► 2 Corinthians 5:17

- ► Philippians 3:13
- ► Devotional reading from *The Love Languages Devotional Bible*, page 1275

TO NEXT DATE

THE AMUSEMENT PARK DATE

34

WORDS TO GROW ON

So I decided there is nothing better than to enjoy food and drink and to find satisfaction in work. Then I realized that these pleasures are from the hand of God.

ECCLESIASTES 2:24

I am suggesting that you live in the present rather than the future. Leave the future joys for future accomplishments. Enjoy today what you have today.

GARY CHAPMAN

SET THE SCENE

What kind of prompting do you need to go on a date to an amusement park? Think about it. With just the two of you to worry about, you can move at your own pace. You can do the things *only you two* want to do and not worry about trying to please an entire group . . . and

you can experience all of the excitement, thrills, fresh air, cotton candy, and fun that you want!

MAKE IT HAPPEN

Once you've settled on an amusement park for your date, check out the following tips for enjoying your day together.

1 *Compromise.*
If you and your date are both hardcore, fearless adrenaline junkies, you can jump on any ride you like without a second thought. If, on the other hand, one of you is somewhat *less* than fearless when it comes to rides, you'll need to take that into account when you choose your rides. Your Amusement Park Date won't be very amusing if one of you is in constant terror. Choose rides you are both comfortable with.

2 *Resolve to try something new.*
On the other hand, your Amusement Park Date is a great time for you to step out of your comfort zone and trust God. If you have a fear of heights or speed or spinning, try a ride that makes you just a little nervous!

3 *Keep your eyes open.*
An amusement park is a prime location for people watching. Take some time between rides—or while you're standing in line—to observe and discuss your fellow park-goers. What can you tell by looking at them—or by the way they interact with others? If you're comfortable with the idea, you might say a quick prayer for people who make an impression on you.

4 *Reminisce.*
Did you spend time in amusement parks as a kid? If so, what was your favorite park? What were your favorite rides? What are your favorite memories of those times? Did you ever get sick or have any misadventures? Swap stories with each other.

5 *Know when to say when.*
If one or both of you starts to drag, don't be afraid to call it a day. Better to end on a high note and preserve good memories than to press your luck and end with crankiness or tired annoyance with each other.

FINISH STRONG

Before you end your Amusement Park Date, spend a few minutes talking about the experience. Use the following questions as needed to guide your discussion.

► How well do we maintain a spirit of joy, fun, and excitement in our daily lives? Explain.

► What are some things that rob us of our joy?

► How does our spirit and attitude reflect on the God we worship?

 ## MIND YOUR LANGUAGE

If your date's primary language is Physical Touch, make sure you offer plenty of it during your time in the park. In addition to walking through the park hand in hand (or with your arms around each other), look for rides that provide opportunities to be close to your special someone. Even better, let your date know those are the rides you're *looking* for.

If you're feeling adventurous, you might want to make a game of your physical touch. Try clasping hands with your date at the beginning of a ride—ideally, a roller coaster with a variety of twists, turns, and loops—and seeing if you can make it to the end without letting go.

 ## TAKE IT TO GOD

Before your date, spend some time in prayer as a couple. Thank God for the opportunities you have to enjoy fun and excitement. Ask Him to

- ▶ bless your time together;
- ▶ keep you safe from harm;
- ▶ give you a renewed sense of excitement and fun in your everyday life.

DIG DEEP

The Bible has a lot to say about enjoying life. Here are a few passages to get you started.

- ▶ Proverbs 17:22
- ▶ Ecclesiastes 5:18
- ▶ Ecclesiastes 11:9
- ▶ John 16:24

- ▶ 1 Timothy 6:17
- ▶ Devotional reading from *The Love Languages Devotional Bible*, page 1013

TO NEXT DATE

THE FIREHOUSE PANCAKE BREAKFAST DATE

35

WORDS TO GROW ON

God has given each of you a gift from his great variety of spiritual gifts. Use them well to serve one another.

1 PETER 4:10

What is the biblical pattern for decision making? The conversation between Jesus and His Father that occurred in Gethsemane just prior to His crucifixion shows the ideal. Jesus humbly prayed, "My Father! If it is possible, let this cup of suffering be taken away from me. Yet I want your will to be done, not mine" (Matthew 26:39). The pattern shows a discussion of ideas and feelings—expressed in honesty and love—with the Father as the recognized leader. The objective is always oneness in our decisions—which the Trinity does perfectly, in every decision.

GARY CHAPMAN

SET THE SCENE

Here's a chance to spend quality time with your sweetheart, doing something nice for the men and women of your local fire department, and working on your decision-making skills as a couple. The Firehouse Pancake Breakfast Date is a way to say thank you to your local first responders—people who would risk their lives to save yours.

MAKE IT HAPPEN

The Firehouse Pancake Breakfast Date is perhaps the most ambitious idea in this book. Are you up for the challenge? If you commit to the task and promise each other you will prioritize making decisions together, you could go a long way toward establishing some vital connections and relationships in your community.

The first thing you'll need to do is answer some important questions.

▶ Do you and your significant other want to tackle it alone—or would you prefer to recruit some friends, family members, or church members to help you?

▶ What date and time will work best—for you and for the firefighters?

▶ Will you be able to use the kitchen facilities in the firehouse?

▶ How many firefighters will you be feeding?

▶ Are there any dietary needs you should be aware of?

Once you have the logistics figured out, begin planning the date—or dates, since the preparation will probably take a day or two. You'll need to shop for ingredients, of course.

Consider bringing some mementos for the firefighters. For example, you might recruit a children's Sunday school class at church to make thank-you cards. Whatever you do, make sure to spearhead the effort together. After you finish cooking breakfast, talk to the firefighters about their lives and families. Ask them how you and other people in your community can assist them. Work to build a relationship with them that lasts far beyond your morning meal.

FINISH STRONG

Before you end your Firehouse Pancake Breakfast Date, spend a few minutes talking with each other about the experience. Use the following questions as needed to guide your discussion.

- ▶ What's the most significant thing that happened this morning?

- ▶ What will we do differently next time?

- ▶ How, specifically, can we use our spiritual gifts to serve others in our community?

MIND YOUR LANGUAGE

If your date's primary love language is Receiving Gifts, see if you can score a memento of your Firehouse Pancake Breakfast Date. The ideal gift would be a T-shirt or sweatshirt with the fire department name and logo on it. If that's not available, take a group picture of the firefighters posing with your significant other in front of the fire station. Have the photo framed, and present it to your date as a souvenir.

TAKE IT TO GOD

Before your date, spend some time in prayer as a couple. Thank God for the brave men and women who protect and serve your community every day. Ask God to

- ▶ bless your efforts to give something back to them so that it's received in the spirit in which it's offered;

- ▶ bring you and your significant other closer together as you prepare for your Firehouse Pancake Breakfast Date;

- ▶ protect the first responders from harm as they go about their duties.

DIG DEEP

You'll find a wealth of verses in Scripture that talk about the importance of serving others. Here are just a few.

- ▶ Mark 10:44–45
- ▶ John 13:12–14
- ▶ Acts 20:35
- ▶ Galatians 5:13–14

- ▶ Philippians 2:1–11
- ▶ Devotional reading from *The Love Languages Devotional Bible*, page 1045

THE PHOTOGRAPHY DATE

WORDS TO GROW ON

*Don't be concerned about the outward beauty
of fancy hairstyles, expensive jewelry, or beautiful
clothes. You should clothe yourselves instead
with the beauty that comes from within,
the unfading beauty of a gentle and quiet spirit,
which is so precious to God.*

1 PETER 3:3–4

*If you struggle with inferiority feelings, rest
assured that 99 percent of the people who know
you perceive you to be smarter, more attractive,
and of greater value than you see yourself.*

GARY CHAPMAN

SET THE SCENE

All you need for the Photography Date is a camera
and two willing subjects. This is an opportunity
for you to capture images that reflect the beauty
you see in each other. If you refuse to let camera

shyness or self-consciousness get in the way of that opportunity, you may be pleasantly surprised by the results.

MAKE IT HAPPEN

You'll need a camera and an artistic vision (or at least an idea of how you want your significant other to look). Beyond that, the details of the Photography Date are up to you. Here a few tips you might consider.

1 *Try a variety of settings.*
Take some pictures of each other in familiar surroundings—relaxing in a favorite room of your house, working in the garden, participating in a favorite pastime, or doing something else you love. Contrast those with some pictures in unconventional settings.

2 *Think outside the portrait box.*
Sure, you'll want to get some standard portraits of each other. But don't stop there. Try some unusual angles or perspectives. Get a close-up of your date's hand or eyes. Use some unconventional lighting techniques. Get creative. Make these photos your own.

3 *Get candid.*
Take your camera to a church function, a family dinner, or a get-together with friends. Get some shots without your date knowing. Capture your interactions with others.

4 *Keep a positive attitude.*
Consider establishing a "No Self-Deprecation Rule" throughout the day. That is, neither one of you is allowed

to complain nor say anything negative about the way you think you look.

Keep in mind that the picture-taking is only the first part of the date. The second part is to look at and talk about the fruits of your labor. Make a slideshow of your photos and watch it together. Talk about the pictures—what you see in each one, what it reveals about the other person, why you took it. Consider posting the best photos to your Facebook or Instagram page.

FINISH STRONG

Before you end your Photography Date, spend a few minutes talking about the experience. Use the following questions as needed to guide your discussion.

- ▶ If each of us could see ourselves through the other person's eyes, what effect would it have on our self-image?

- ▶ Why does God put most of our *really* good qualities on the inside?

- ▶ How can we learn to focus on the good qualities inside other people?

MIND YOUR LANGUAGE

By the end of your Photography Date, you should have dozens of pictures of each other. Why not print your favorites and put them in a photo album? If your date's primary love language is Receiving Gifts, the work you put into the album will feel like love to him or her.

If you really want to create a memorable gift, add some photographer's notes to the album. In just a few sentences, explain what each photo means to you—what you were thinking when you took it, what it reveals about the other person, and why it should be preserved in an album.

 ## TAKE IT TO GOD
Before your date, spend some time in prayer with each other. Thank God for the beauty of His creation. Thank Him specifically for the beauty—inner and outer—that you see in each other. Ask God to

- ▶ bless your time together on your Photography Date;
- ▶ help you create an atmosphere in which you both feel comfortable about having your picture taken;
- ▶ help you come away from your date feeling appreciated and affirmed.

DIG DEEP

The Bible contains quite a few passages that could apply to your Photography Date. Here are a few you may want to check out.

- ▶ 1 Samuel 16:7
- ▶ Psalm 34:5
- ▶ Psalm 139:14
- ▶ Proverbs 31:30

- ▶ Song of Songs 4:7
- ▶ Devotional reading from *The Love Languages Devotional Bible*, page 161

TO NEXT DATE

THE FOOD PANTRY DATE

WORDS TO GROW ON

*For I was hungry, and you fed me. I was thirsty,
and you gave me a drink. I was a stranger,
and you invited me into your home.*

MATTHEW 25:35

*Jesus once said, "It is more blessed to give
than to receive" (Acts 20:35 NIV). It is the
blessing that we want family members to
experience. If serving others is in fact a virtue,
then it will bring its own internal reward.*

GARY CHAPMAN

SET THE SCENE

Jesus said when we care for the hungry, thirsty,
naked, sick, or imprisoned, we are actually caring
for Him. That's how closely He identifies with
hurting people.

For better or worse, there is no shortage of
opportunities to show our love for Jesus by caring

for people in need—especially those who are hungry. Statistics show that there are more than fifty million people in the United States alone who face food insecurity—that is, they don't know where their next meal will come from.

God established a network to prevent people from falling through the cracks. It's called the body of Christ. As part of that body, we have a responsibility to care for those in need—to make their problems our problems. During your Food Pantry Date, you'll have a chance to make a difference in other people's lives alongside the person who's made a difference in yours.

MAKE IT HAPPEN

The first thing you'll need to do on your Food Pantry Date is become acquainted with your local food pantry (assuming you're not already acquainted with it). Make arrangements to tour the facility as a couple. Get a good sense of how it operates. When you leave, take with you a list of items that are most needed at the pantry. From there, the two of you can decide how you'll spend your Food Pantry Date.

One option is to spend an afternoon raising awareness of the food pantry. Design and print out some fliers. Go door-to-door in your area, handing out the fliers, explaining where the pantry is and how it serves the community, and answering any questions people may have.

If you're uncomfortable with that idea, you could simply spend your date shopping for food—and brainstorming other ways you could help out at the pantry.

FINISH STRONG

Before you end your Food Pantry Date, spend a few minutes talking about the experience. Use the following questions as needed to guide your discussion.

- ▶ What, specifically, is our God-given responsibility to people who are hurting and in need?

- ▶ What are some of the things that get in the way of that responsibility?

- ▶ What steps can we take to become more involved in the lives of people in need?

MIND YOUR LANGUAGE

If your date's primary love language is Quality Time, consider repeating your Food Pantry Date once a week. Set aside an hour or two every week to collect food, stock shelves, take inventory, do publicity, or assist in distributing the food at your local food pantry.

Working side by side with your significant other every week for an hour or two will go a long way toward filling your sweetheart's love tank. And it will be a blessing to many.

TAKE IT TO GOD

Before your date, spend some time in prayer with each other. Praise God for the fact that He cares deeply about people in need. Praise Him for using the body of Christ to accomplish His work on earth. Thank Him for the opportunity to share in that work as a member of the body of Christ. Ask Him to

- ▶ bless your efforts to serve others—to use the food you collect or distribute to make a difference in the lives of people in need;

- ▶ help you maintain a spirit of humility and gratitude for the opportunity to do His work;

- ▶ help you expand your role in the local food pantry ministry and make it part of your life.

DIG DEEP

The Bible makes it clear that God's people have a responsibility to care for those in need. Here are a few passages you may want to check out.

- ▶ Proverbs 28:27
- ▶ Isaiah 58:10
- ▶ Luke 3:11
- ▶ Romans 12:20

- ▶ James 2:14–18
- ▶ Devotional reading from *The Love Languages Devotional Bible*, page 396

THE GAME NIGHT DATE

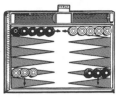

WORDS TO GROW ON

A glad heart makes a happy face;
a broken heart crushes the spirit.

PROVERBS 15:13

All of us blossom when we feel loved,
and wither when we do not feel loved.

GARY CHAPMAN

SET THE SCENE

Board games are one of life's simple pleasures. You don't need 3-D graphics or motion-sensor technology to enjoy them. Plastic tokens, maybe a pair of dice, and a square piece of cardboard blocked out in colorfully strategic ways offer hours of entertainment—and time to talk.

Board games are also great equalizers. You don't have to be athletically gifted in order to do well. As a result, even people who aren't naturally competitive can get caught up in no-holds-barred games of Monopoly or Sorry.

For some, board games are a link to the past. They evoke memories of childhood—of sitting around a table with their parents or grandparents, saying things like, "I think Colonel Mustard did it with a lead pipe in the conservatory." (Let's hear it for Clue.)

For those reasons and more, a Game Night Date may be just the thing your relationship needs.

MAKE IT HAPPEN

If either of you has board games at home, pull out a few of your favorites for a nice, relaxed evening of light competition and heavy fun. If your game inventory is low, borrow a game or two from your friends. If possible, find some that are specifically geared to two players (Battleship or Stratego, for example).

Ideally your Game Night Date will consist of equal parts game play and relaxed conversation. Talk freely about whatever topics occur to you. Enjoy your time together.

Resist the urge to play video games during your date. Most video games are solitary pursuits. Even multiplayer games require you to face the screen, instead of each other. Because of the fast-moving nature of the games, your attention is necessarily focused on game play. The opportunities for conversation and interaction with each other about something other than the game are minimal.

Keep in mind, too, that competition isn't the point of the date. Winning should be the furthest thing from your mind. If you're an ultracompetitive person by nature, make sure you curb your impulses for your Game Night Date. Celebrate each other's victories and downplay your own. And if a game drags on past the point of enjoyment, don't hesitate to call it a draw and move on to the next one.

FINISH STRONG

Before you end your Game Night Date, spend a few minutes talking about the experience. Use the following questions as needed to guide your discussion.

- ► What was the best thing about our Game Night Date?

- ► Agree or disagree? We should spend more quiet evenings at home like this. Why?

- ► In what other ways do we need to "quiet" our lives so that we can hear God's voice?

MIND YOUR LANGUAGE

If your date's primary love language is Words of Affirmation, your Game Night Date offers an ideal opportunity to fill his or her tank. Your strategy is simple: to offer as many compliments and words of affirmation as possible to your significant other without sounding insincere.

The obstacle standing in your way is cynicism. If your efforts are too transparent or too forced, your loved one may get suspicious, in which case the effect will be ruined. Your challenge, then, is to offer *sincere* words of affirmation that make them feel loved and appreciated.

TAKE IT TO GOD

Before your date, spend some time in prayer as a couple. Thank God for the opportunity to enjoy a fun, worry-free evening together. Ask Him to

- ▶ bless the time you spend together during your Game Night Date;

- ▶ help you maintain a lighthearted attitude and not get caught up in matters of winning or losing;

- ▶ guide your conversation during your date so that something good and meaningful comes from it.

DIG DEEP

You can find many passages in Scripture that fit the theme of your Game Night Date. Here are a few to get you started.

- ▶ Deuteronomy 12:7

- ▶ Ecclesiastes 2:24

- ▶ Ecclesiastes 3:1–13

- ▶ Ecclesiastes 8:15

- ▶ Ecclesiastes 11:9

- ▶ Devotional reading from *The Love Languages Devotional Bible*, page 844

TO NEXT DATE

THE BIKE RIDE DATE

WORDS TO GROW ON

*We also pray that you will be strengthened
with all his glorious power so you will have
all the endurance and patience you need.
May you be filled with joy.*

COLOSSIANS 1:11

*For love, we will climb mountains, cross seas,
traverse desert sands, and endure untold
hardships. Without love, mountains become
unclimbable, seas uncrossable, deserts
unbearable, and hardships our lot in life.*

GARY CHAPMAN

SET THE SCENE

For some people, a "Bike Ride Date" conjures
up images of a leisurely ride through the neighborhood or to the ice cream store and back.
And that's fine, if health or a lack of biking
experience (or confidence) is an issue.

If, on the other hand, you both are physically and experientially equipped to push your endurance on your bikes—to power your way across dozens of miles of challenging terrain—you'll find extra meaning in this date. You'll open the door to a conversation about the endurance that's required for successful relationships—with each other and with Christ.

MAKE IT HAPPEN

The specifics of your Bike Ride Date will depend on your location and your experience level on a bike. There are a few tips, however, that you'll need to keep in mind as you plan the date.

1 *Know exactly where—and how far—you're going.*
Plot your course carefully, especially if one (or both) of you is a cycling novice. You can find a variety of cycling sites online that will help you plan a route.

A good rule of thumb for distance is that you never plan a ride that's longer than 50 percent more than your previous longest ride. If you've never ridden more than twelve miles together, don't plan a trip that's longer than eighteen miles.

2 *Make sure you're ready to go.*
Polish your mechanical skills before the trip. Make sure you know how to properly change a flat tire or fix a broken chain.

You'll also need to dress appropriately. Avoid cotton clothing, which absorbs moisture and causes chafing and blisters. Opt instead for padded chamois bike shorts made from antimicrobial fabric. Your body will thank you.

Stay hydrated and nourished. A good rule of thumb is to drink before you get thirsty and eat before you get hungry.

You'll need to bring plenty of water, as well as quick snacks such as food bars, gels, trail mix, and Fig Newtons.

3 *Make sure your bike is in optimal working order.*
Check your tire pressure before your ride. Clean and lube your chains, and make sure your seat is correctly positioned.

4 *Be a road rules follower.*
Hold your line while you ride. Stay in your lane. Stay off the shoulder of the road. Obey traffic signals and signs. Act like you're driving a car. (For more information about cycling safety, check your state's Department of Transportation website.)

FINISH STRONG

Before you end your Bike Ride Date, spend a few minutes talking as a couple about the experience. Use the following questions as needed to guide your discussion.

- ► Why is endurance important in a relationship?
- ► Why is it important in our Christian walk?
- ► What are some specific things we can do to help each other build relational and spiritual endurance?

 ## MIND YOUR LANGUAGE
If your date's primary love language is Acts of Service, you can fill their love tank by preparing their bike for the trip. If you have the skills and experience to do the work yourself, have at it. If not, leave the task to your local bike shop.

TAKE IT TO GOD

Before your date, spend some time in prayer together. Ask God to

- ▶ bless your time together;
- ▶ keep you free from harm on your bike ride;
- ▶ help you recognize the importance of endurance—in your relationship and in your Christian walk.

DIG DEEP

The Bible contains several passages that encourage us to build our endurance and stamina so that we can enjoy the full range of experiences the Christian life brings. Here are a few to get you started.

- ▶ Romans 5:3–4
- ▶ Romans 12:12
- ▶ 1 Corinthians 10:13
- ▶ Hebrews 10:36

- ▶ James 1:12–18
- ▶ Devotional reading from *The Love Languages Devotional Bible*, page 63

TO NEXT DATE

THE FLEA MARKET DATE

WORDS TO GROW ON

*Then he said, "Beware! Guard against
every kind of greed. Life is not measured
by how much you own."*

LUKE 12:15

*Real satisfaction is not found in money,
but in righteousness, godliness, faith, love,
endurance, and gentleness—in short, living
with God and according to His values.*

GARY CHAPMAN

SET THE SCENE

You don't have to enjoy shopping to have a good
time at a flea market. The experience is often
more like an archaeological expedition than a
shopping trip. You can uncover artifacts and
meet people at a flea market that you wouldn't
encounter anywhere else. That's why it makes a
great setting for a date.

If you're so inclined, a flea market can be a great place for contemplation, too. Here's a sample topic ripe for mulling over. Their owners once considered many of the personal items for sale at a flea market valuable. Now they can be had for a few dollars. What does that say about the things we consider valuable? What would God say about those things?

That's just one of the many lively discussions you can have with each other on your Flea Market Date.

MAKE IT HAPPEN

The best way to explore a flea market is in a relaxed, unhurried, leisurely manner. So if your schedule allows it, block out an entire morning or afternoon for your Flea Market Date. A quick online search should give you the location and hours of operation of flea markets in your area.

If you're not a shopper by nature, you may need to do some self-talk before your date to get into a proper frame of mind. In this case, patience is not just a virtue; it's a key to success for your date.

While you enjoy the wonders of the flea market, engage each other in various topics of conversation. Talk about the things you see, the people who stand out, the memories that are sparked— anything that comes to mind. Refer back to the "Set the Scene" and "Take It to God" sections for other discussion ideas.

If you want to add some extra excitement to your day, try tackling one of the following flea market challenges:

▶ Find something for less than $10 that really means something to you.

- See which one of you can find the gaudiest article of clothing for sale.

- See which one of you can find the oldest item for sale.

- Find an item that is an exact duplicate of something you once owned.

- Find the perfect item to commemorate your date.

Better yet, come up with some challenges of your own.

FINISH STRONG

Before you end your Flea Market Date, spend a few minutes talking with each other about the experience. Use the following questions as needed to guide your discussion.

- Why are earthly treasures so tempting?

- How can we tell when we're putting too much emphasis on earthly treasures?

- What specific steps can we take to keep our eyes focused on heavenly treasures?

MIND YOUR LANGUAGE

If your significant other's primary love language is Physical Touch, spend your day at the flea market filling her love tank. Look for opportunities to

- hold her hand while you walk;

- sneak a kiss when no one is looking;

- put your arms around her while she's examining a seller's wares;

▶ help her try on goofy hats and sunglasses.

Feel free to add your own ideas to the list. Just make sure your sweetheart comes away from your Flea Market Date feeling especially loved.

TAKE IT TO GOD

Before your date, spend some time in prayer together. Thank God for the opportunity to spend time with each other in a relaxed setting. Ask Him to

- ▶ bless the time you spend together so that He may be glorified by it;

- ▶ guide your discussion about the "treasures" (material possessions) that seem valuable to us;

- ▶ help you examine the prevailing attitude in your household toward possessions.

DIG DEEP

Looking for more Bible passages that fit the theme of your Flea Market Date? Try these.

- ▶ Matthew 6:19–21
- ▶ Matthew 16:26
- ▶ 1 Timothy 6:10
- ▶ 1 John 2:16

- ▶ 1 John 3:17
- ▶ Devotional reading from *The Love Languages Devotional Bible,* page 235

TO NEXT DATE

THE SECOND FIRST DATE

WORDS TO GROW ON

*Many waters cannot quench love,
nor can rivers drown it. If a man tried to
buy love with all his wealth, his offer
would be utterly scorned.*

SONG OF SONGS 8:7

*If you give [God] the opportunity, [He]
will not only show the two of you the way
to walk but He will also give you the
power to take the necessary steps.*

GARY CHAPMAN

SET THE SCENE

How much do you remember about the first
time you went out with your significant other?
Did you go by yourselves, or was it a double
date or group date? Where did you go? If it was
a restaurant, what did you order? Did you go
to a movie afterward? What did you see? Who

chose it? Did you both enjoy it? How long did the date last? What were you both wearing?

What was the chemistry like on that first date? Were you both nervous? Did the conversation flow freely—or did you suffer through awkward silences? What were your first impressions of each other? Did you sense right away that there was something special between you?

The more of these questions you can answer, the more successful your Second First Date will be. As the name suggests, the object is to re-create, as faithfully as possible, your first date with your sweetheart.

MAKE IT HAPPEN

Needless to say, preparation is key for this date. The more you put into it, the better chance you have of crafting a masterpiece. If you can get key details right in re-creating your first date, you can expect a memorable time together.

Do you still have the clothes you wore on that date? If not, can you find something similar? Can you still go to the places you went that day? If not, can you go to the places that are on those sites now and reminisce? Can you make a playlist of songs you might have heard?

Re-create what you can physically. Fill in the rest with your memories of that date. Use every bit of your imagination and creativity to let your date know how much that first activity together meant to you in the grand scheme of your life.

FINISH STRONG

Before you end your Second First Date, spend a few minutes talking with each other about the experience. Use the following questions as needed to guide your discussion.

- ▶ Why did the Lord bring us together?
- ▶ What might He accomplish in and through our relationship?
- ▶ How can we make sure we stay receptive to His will in our lives?

MIND YOUR LANGUAGE

If your significant other's primary love language is Acts of Service, the Second First Date offers a prime opportunity to fill his or her love tank. In advance of your date, make a list of the friends, family members, coworkers, and acquaintances that were part of your life the first time the two of you went out. Think of the people you talked to about your date or the people who weighed in on your burgeoning relationship.

Contact as many of those people as possible, explain your idea for a Second First Date, and ask them to share some of their memories of that date—or of the early days of your relationship. One way to do that is to post something on your favorite social media site and invite friends to offer their comments. You can use their feedback to enhance the date experience for you both.

TAKE IT TO GOD

Before your date, spend some time in prayer as a couple. Thank God for the unique way He brought the two of you together. Thank Him for the countless blessings He's bestowed on your relationship. See how many of those blessings you can name. Ask God to

- ▶ sharpen your memory to help you recall the significant details of your first date;

- ▶ help you maintain a spirit of thankfulness for your relationship throughout your Second First Date;

- ▶ help you recognize that your past experiences have prepared and equipped you for the future plans He has for you.

DIG DEEP

In the spirit of remembering the Lord's goodness, here are a few Bible verses for you to check out.

- ▶ Luke 12:22–31
- ▶ 2 Corinthians 9:8–10
- ▶ Philippians 2:12–13
- ▶ Philippians 4:19

- ▶ James 1:17
- ▶ Devotional reading from *The Love Languages Devotional Bible*, page 655

THE PEOPLE-WATCHING DATE

42

WORDS TO GROW ON

*Dear friends, let us continue to love one another,
for love comes from God. Anyone who loves is a
child of God and knows God. But anyone who
does not love does not know God, for God is love.*

1 JOHN 4:7–8

*In Western culture, isolation is seen as one
of the most stringent of punishments. Even
criminals do not aspire to solitary confinement.*

GARY CHAPMAN

SET THE SCENE

The People-Watching Date gives you an
opportunity to observe and celebrate the diversity
of God's human creation. No two snowflakes
are alike? Bah. No two *humans* are alike. All are
equally fascinating in their own way. Sometimes
you just need to look closely to see it.

Spending a few hours in a public setting, watching all manner of human activity and interaction, can affect not only your mood but also your outlook on life—especially if you tend to be an introvert. Being able to share the experience—and trade observations with your spouse—further increases that effect.

MAKE IT HAPPEN

You can turn a simple people-watching expedition into an epic date. You just need to remember three important tips.

1 *Choose the right location.*
Any place a crowd gathers is a great place for people watching. The public setting you choose will determine the type of sights you see. People watching at an airport, for example, lends itself to more dramatic tableaus—family members saying goodbye to loved ones, businesspeople venting their frustrations toward security personnel, harried travelers trying to make connecting flights. Consider the type of watching you'd like to do before you settle on a location.

2 *Practice your furtive glances.*
Rule #1 for people watching is *don't get caught.* No one likes to be stared at (well, almost no one). If people get the sense that you're spying on them, it may lead to some unpleasant confrontations. And who needs that on a date?

Keep your glances quick and casual. Perfect the art of watching people without their knowing that you're watching them.

3 *Don't be content merely to watch.*
What do you do if you see someone who looks especially interesting, intriguing, or friendly? You introduce yourselves,

of course. You're not doing clinical research. There are no rules prohibiting interaction between watchers and watchees.

Transform your People-Watching Date into a People-Meeting Date. Offer a compliment. Ask a polite, nonintrusive question. Strike up a conversation. More often than not, total strangers will welcome dialogue with friendly people.

Who knows? Maybe you'll come away from your People-Watching Date with a refreshed relationship *and* a new friend.

FINISH STRONG

Before you end your People-Watching Date, spend a few minutes talking about the experience. Use the following questions as needed to guide your discussion.

- ▶ What can we learn about people from watching them in a public setting?

- ▶ What conclusions might people draw about us if they saw us in a public setting?

- ▶ What can we do to make a difference in the lives of people we don't know?

MIND YOUR LANGUAGE

If your loved one's primary love language is Words of Affirmation, use your interactions with the people you meet during your People-Watching Date to fill his or her love tank. Take every opportunity to talk up your significant other, without being obnoxious about it, of course. Leave no doubt in the minds of the people you encounter as to how you feel about your loved one.

In the process, you'll leave your date feeling loved and affirmed.

TAKE IT TO GOD

Before your date, spend some time in prayer as a couple. Thank God for the variety of people He puts in your life every day—people to interact with and learn from, people to influence and be influenced by. Ask Him to

- ▶ bless your time together on your People-Watching Date;

- ▶ guide your interactions with the people you see and meet so that He will be glorified through those encounters;

- ▶ help you make a positive influence on other people's lives during the course of your People-Watching Date.

DIG DEEP

The Bible has quite a bit to say about showing love and concern for others. Here's just a sampling.

- ▶ John 13:34–35
- ▶ 1 Corinthians 13:1–13
- ▶ Colossians 3:12–15
- ▶ Hebrews 13:1–25

- ▶ 1 Peter 4:8
- ▶ Devotional reading from *The Love Languages Devotional Bible,* page 1092

THE BACKRUB DATE

WORDS TO GROW ON

*Share each other's burdens,
and in this way obey the law of Christ.*

GALATIANS 6:2

*God became human in order to touch us.
In Scripture, we find Him touching children,
those afflicted with leprosy, the blind and
the deaf. His touch brought healing and
hope to everyone He encountered.*

GARY CHAPMAN

SET THE SCENE

Life is filled with stressors and tension. The
deadlines, expectations, setbacks, and obstacles
we face every day can weigh heavily on our
shoulders—in a very real, physical sense. The
more those stressors build up, the greater the
tension and discomfort we feel.

How would you like to be an instrument of relief and comfort for your significant other? That's what the Backrub Date is all about.

With a few practiced movements of your hands, fingers, and thumbs, you can rub the tension from your date's shoulders and back. You can work the stress out of her muscles. You can help him relax and feel at ease. You can improve the way she feels.

And when you're done . . . you may receive a similar treatment. Everyone wins on a Backrub Date!

MAKE IT HAPPEN

Of all the dates in this book, the Backrub Date is probably the closest to a sure winner. Who doesn't love a backrub? Here are a few tips to help you maximize the experience.

1 *Go to backrub school.* You don't actually have to enroll in a class. You can find hundreds of how-to massage demonstrations online—some of which actually feature professionals. You can also find a plethora of books on the topic at your local library or bookstore. See if you can  pick up some workable techniques that will serve you—and your date—well.

2 *First do no harm.*
Unless you're a licensed physical therapist, don't try to give each other massage therapy for an injury or a medical condition. Likewise, be careful when you're trying to work out "kinks" in each other's muscles.

3 *Set the proper mood.*
For maximum results, your approach to relaxation and stress relief must be holistic. Make sure the massage table (or couch or floor or whatever you use) is comfortable. Make sure your room is free from distractions (or reminders of daily pressures). Light some candles. Play some soothing background music.

4 *Remind yourself that it's better to give than receive.*
Ideally your Backrub Date will end with you both having received long, relaxing massages. However, receiving a massage must not be your aim. If your sweetheart senses that you're just going through the motions while you wait for your own massage, she may have trouble relaxing. Prepare to spend the bulk of your Backrub Date in giving mode. Anything your date does for you, then, will be icing on the cake.

FINISH STRONG

Before you end your Backrub Date, spend a few minutes talking about the experience. Use the following questions as needed to guide your discussion.

▶ What are the biggest sources of tension and stress in your life right now?

- Why does God allow you to face such difficult situations?

- In addition to backrubs, what are some God-honoring ways you can help each other deal with tension and stress?

MIND YOUR LANGUAGE

If your date's primary love language is Physical Touch, you could go a long way toward keeping his or her love tank full by scheduling weekly backrub sessions. Find a time on your calendar that works for both of you. Set it aside for a backrub session so you can show Physical Touch on a regular basis.

TAKE IT TO GOD

Before your date, spend some time in prayer together. Thank God for caring about your health—both spiritual and emotional. Thank Him for giving you a friend who helps you restore equilibrium and sanity when the pressures of the world get to be too much. Ask God to

- bless your time together during your Backrub Date;

- help you provide comfort, relaxation, and stress relief to each other;

- equip you to deal with the tension and pressures of daily life in a healthy way.

DIG DEEP

You can find a variety of verses in Scripture that talk about helping and comforting others. Here are just a few.

- Luke 6:38
- John 15:12
- 2 Corinthians 1:3–4
- Philippians 2:4

- Hebrews 6:10
- Devotional reading from *The Love Languages Devotional Bible*, page 38

THE TREE-PLANTING DATE

WORDS TO GROW ON

*But blessed are those who trust in the Lord and
have made the Lord their hope and confidence.
They are like trees planted along a riverbank,
with roots that reach deep into the water.
Such trees are not bothered by the heat or
worried by long months of drought. Their leaves
stay green, and they never stop producing fruit.*

JEREMIAH 17:7–8

*Learning how to help each other process emotions
is a part of growing a healthy dating relationship.*

GARY CHAPMAN

SET THE SCENE

Imagine having a living symbol of your relationship,
one that grows and matures and changes with the sea-
sons of life, one that is a reminder to you both of your
relationship. Imagine taking comfort or strength from
the elm in your backyard or the oak in a local park.

Pretty heady results from a single day's work, but why not give it a shot? If you invest your time and energy in a Tree-Planting Date, you'll reap dividends for years to come.

MAKE IT HAPPEN

Keep in mind that your Tree-Planting Date isn't some half-baked grade school Arbor Day project. You're not going to throw some seeds in a hole and hope for the best. If you want a tree that will mature and thrive for decades to come, you need to exercise due diligence in your planting.

1 *Take care of the preliminaries.*
In order to determine what tree is right for you, you first need to decide what the tree's purpose will be (aside from standing as a testament to your relationship). If married, are you trying to beautify your yard? Do you want it to provide privacy? Are you looking to reduce your cooling costs through the shade the tree will provide? Are you planting a tree for someone else?

After you've determined the tree's purpose, determine the geography and weather of your planting site. Note any height restrictions due to utility lines, sun exposure, and soil conditions.

2 *Find the right tree.*
If you're planting a bare-root seedling, a balled-and-burlapped tree, or one that's been potted, you can find detailed advice for making sure your tree is healthy at various online gardening sites. If you're transplanting a mature tree, you'll want to make sure its

▶ bark is healthy;

- trunk and limbs are free from insect infestation or mechanical damage;
- branches are well distributed.

3 *Plant it correctly.*
Obviously the planting process is a little more involved than dig hole, insert tree, and cover hole. Different types of trees require different methods of planting. Talk to your local nursery about the nuances of getting your tree in the ground.

4 *Mulch, mulch, mulch.*
Mulch is a fledgling tree's best friend. Make sure you have enough mulch to surround the tree to a diameter of at least three feet. It should also be 3–4 inches deep.

5 *Talk to the experts.*
After your tree is in the ground, you'll need to learn how to water it, prune it, and keep it safe from insects and disease. Your best bet, then, is to foster a relationship with the employees of your local nursery.

FINISH STRONG

Before you end your Tree-Planting Date, spend a few minutes talking about the experience. Use the following questions as needed to guide your discussion.

- What will this tree need in order to survive and thrive?
- What will our relationship need in order to survive and thrive along with it?
- What will this tree symbolize?

MIND YOUR LANGUAGE

If your significant other's primary love language is Acts of Service, you can make a strong impression by creating a plaque to commemorate the planting of your tree. It doesn't need to be anything fancy—just something with your names and the date (and maybe a heart) on it that will mark the event.

TAKE IT TO GOD

Before your date, spend some time in prayer together. Thank God for allowing your relationship to grow and for giving it the strength to withstand storms. Ask Him to bless

- ▶ your time with each other;
- ▶ your efforts to plant your tree;
- ▶ the continued growth and maturity of both the tree and your relationship.

DIG DEEP

You can find several passages in God's Word that talk about trees and growing strong in the Lord. Start with these ideas.

- ▶ Job 14:7
- ▶ Psalm 1:3
- ▶ Proverbs 13:12
- ▶ Daniel 4:10–12
- ▶ Matthew 7:17

- ▶ Devotional reading from *The Love Languages Devotional Bible,* page 1121

THE MEMORY LANE DATE

WORDS TO GROW ON

*We have happy memories of the godly, but
the name of a wicked person rots away.*

PROVERBS 10:7

45

*One of the by-products of quality activities is
that they provide a memory bank from which
to draw in the years ahead.*

GARY CHAPMAN

SET THE SCENE

Whether you and your sweetheart have been together
for forty weeks or forty years, your past is ripe for
exploring. Consider the sheer number of memories
you share that bring a smile to your face every time
they cross your mind. Your shared experiences give
your relationship strength and uniqueness.

The Memory Lane Date encourages you to
unpack those memories—to relive your favorite

moments as a couple—using video, photos, or your own recollections.

Living in the past does no one any good. No relationship can thrive by constantly looking backward. But a quick peek—one date spent reminiscing about the days that laid the foundation for your relationship—can be a rejuvenating and refreshing change of pace.

MAKE IT HAPPEN

The Memory Lane Date will work well anytime, but it's especially effective in conjunction with an anniversary. Do it on your wedding anniversary, if you are married, or perhaps the anniversary of your first date or your first kiss or the first time you ever said, "I love you."

You can make the date as intimate or as inclusive as you like. If there are people who've had a front-row seat to your relationship over the years—people whose presence would enhance your date—invite them along. Ask them to share some of their favorite memories of your relationship.

If you'd prefer a more intimate date, plan to go to a place that has significance to your relationship—your old high school, the site of your first date, the church where you got married. If that's not possible, you could simply watch your wedding video, look through old photo albums, or share your favorite memories with each other.

FINISH STRONG

Before you end your Memory Lane Date, spend a few minutes talking with each other about the experience. Use the following questions as needed to guide your discussion.

- Looking back, what were some of the signs that God intended the two of you to be together?

- If you could go back in time and talk to yourselves on your first date, what advice would you give?

- What are some signs that God has big things planned for your future?

MIND YOUR LANGUAGE

If your date's primary love language is Physical Touch, see if you can recreate the first time the two of you ever held hands—or the first time you ever kissed. You don't necessarily have to go to the location where the hand-holding or kissing occurred (unless the idea appeals to both of you). Instead, you can re-create the scene in your living room or backyard.

As you do, talk about how you felt at the time (to the best of your recollection). Were you nervous? Were your hands clammy? Were your lips dry? Were you overcome with emotion? Did you realize it was the start of something big?

Move from the past to the present by talking about how you feel about kissing or holding hands with each other now. What does it mean to you? How is it different now that you've both gotten so good at it?

TAKE IT TO GOD

Before your date, spend some time in prayer together. Thank God for bringing the two of you together. Thank Him for the many blessings He's bestowed on your relationships. (Name as many of those individual blessings as you can recall.) Thank Him for the plans He has for your future. Ask Him to

- help you approach your date with a proper spirit of joy, celebration, and thankfulness;

- bring to mind other blessings in your relationship that you may have forgotten or allowed to pass unnoticed;

- be glorified through the celebration of your Memory Lane Date.

DIG DEEP

The Bible strongly recommends remembering God's blessings and giving thanks for them. Here are some prompts to get you started.

- Psalm 78:4
- Psalm 89:1
- Psalm 103:2
- Psalm 105:5

- Psalm 106:1–2
- Devotional reading from *The Love Languages Devotional Bible,* page 907

TO NEXT DATE

THE ART GALLERY DATE

WORDS TO GROW ON

The Lord has filled Bezalel with the Spirit of God, giving him great wisdom, ability, and expertise in all kinds of crafts. He is a master craftsman, expert in working with gold, silver, and bronze.

EXODUS 35:31–32

God created a being with whom the man could have a face-to-face relationship, an in-depth personal relationship in which the two are united in an unbreakable union that satisfies the deepest longings of the human heart.

GARY CHAPMAN

46

SET THE SCENE

You don't have to be an aficionado of the visual arts to enjoy an Art Gallery Date. All you need is an open mind and an appreciation for God's gift of creativity—in its various forms. Depending on the gallery (or exhibition or museum) you choose, you may be exposed to the works of the masters or of burgeoning local artists. Some works may amuse you; others may confuse you. Some will strike you as profound; others will seem like utter nonsense.

Therein lies the beauty of the Art Gallery Date. The setting allows—and encourages—you to bounce your reactions off each other. Ideally that will lead to conversations about the nature of creativity and the works of art that move—or even disturb you.

MAKE IT HAPPEN

If you're a patron of the arts, you know how to approach an Art Gallery Date (or an Art Exhibition Date or an Art Museum Date—the venue doesn't matter, as long as you're being exposed to art). However, if you're a novice, you may want to consider a few tips.

1 *Start with something familiar and interesting.*
Look first for styles and works that naturally appeal to you, whether they fall into the traditional or nontraditional category. Establish a sense of what you like, and talk about why it appeals to you.

2 *Test your limits.*
Move on to styles and works that don't necessarily appeal to you at first glance. Talk about your reactions to those works. If you and your date disagree about certain works and styles, engage in some friendly debate—without criticizing each other's tastes. Kick around the inevitable question of what constitutes art.

3 *Try your hand.*
Let yourself be inspired by the beauty and creativity you see. Create some works of your own. You may be surprised to find you have artistic talent.

FINISH STRONG

Before you end your Art Gallery Date, spend a few minutes talking about the experience. Use the following questions as needed to guide your discussion.

- ▶ What kind of art means the most to you? Why?

- ▶ What do God's gifts of creativity and artistic ability tell us about Him?

- ▶ How does an appreciation of art—whether it's literature, poetry, songwriting, painting, sculpture, film, stage performance, or something else—enhance our relationship with God? How does it influence our worship?

 ## MIND YOUR LANGUAGE

If your significant other's primary love language is Quality Time, linger with him at the works of art that appeal to him. Spend time carefully examining the pieces. Ask him to tell you why each one catches his eye. Does she prefer a certain medium? A certain style? A certain artist? See if you can learn to appreciate the works as she does.

If your date would prefer not to talk, you can still fill his or her love tank by spending time together in the presence of art that inspires him or her.

TAKE IT TO GOD

Before your date, spend some time in prayer with each other. Thank God for His gift of creativity. Thank Him for the people who make the world a more beautiful place with their art. Thank Him for the artists who challenge us, entertain us, and show us a different way of looking at the world. Ask Him to

- ▶ bless your time together during your Art Gallery Date;
- ▶ help you process and verbalize your reactions to the artwork you see;
- ▶ come away from your date with a deeper appreciation for His gifts of artistry and creativity in each other.

DIG DEEP

As the Creator, God celebrates creativity in His human creation. Here are a few Bible passages that reflect His attitude.

- ▶ Genesis 1:27
- ▶ Exodus 31:1–6
- ▶ Proverbs 22:29
- ▶ Ephesians 2:10

- ▶ Colossians 3:23
- ▶ Devotional reading from *The Love Languages Devotional Bible*, page 444

TO NEXT DATE

THE SKYSCRAPER DATE

47

WORDS TO GROW ON

And we know that God causes everything to work together for the good of those who love God and are called according to his purpose for them.

ROMANS 8:28

As our Sovereign Lord, He will either help us understand His perspective on our situation, or He will ask us simply to trust Him.

GARY CHAPMAN

SET THE SCENE

Sometimes a change of perspective is all you need in order to see things more clearly. That's the notion behind the Skyscraper Date. The object is to get as far above ground level as the architecture in your area will allow.

If you live near a major city, your date may take you to an observation deck more than a hundred stories high. If you live on the outskirts of East

Podunkville, you may have to settle for the roof of the bank building. That's okay. Don't let the title fool you. The key to a successful Skyscraper Date isn't how high you get; it's how willing you are to change your perspective when you get there.

MAKE IT HAPPEN

The one thing you'll need for your Skyscraper Date (aside from a skyscraper—or its local equivalent) is a list of problems, crises, issues, deadlines, and pressures you're facing right now. You and your date may compile separate lists, or you may work together to create a joint one.

Once the two of you are perched above the ground, talk about the things you notice from your new perspective. If you're high enough above street level, things that previously seemed large will appear tiny and insignificant. It's that change of perspective that lies at the heart of this date.

Turn your attention to your list. Talk about how your attitude might change if you looked at those problems, crises, issues, deadlines, and pressures from a different perspective. For example, you might read Romans 8:28 ("And we know that God causes everything to work together for the good of those who love God and are called according to his purpose for them.") and consider how God might be using the trials in your life to accomplish something amazing. Is He giving you much-needed experience? Is He putting you in a place where you can experience a genuine answer to prayer? Is He preparing you to help others in need?

A simple change of perspective may have a profound effect on your outlook.

FINISH STRONG

Before you end your Skyscraper Date, spend a few minutes talking about the experience. Use the following questions as needed to guide your discussion.

- ▶ What are some obstacles that keep us from seeing things from God's perspective?

- ▶ What specific steps can we take to remove those obstacles?

- ▶ How can we encourage each other to look at things from God's perspective?

 ## MIND YOUR LANGUAGE

If your date's primary love language is Words of Affirmation, take a few minutes during your Skyscraper Date to examine your significant other "from a different perspective." Couples who have been together for a while can fall into a rut of taking each other for granted—or, even worse, focusing on each other's annoying habits. Here's your chance to turn things around.

Look at each other from a new perspective—one that notices the other person's good qualities, praiseworthy attributes, or God-given gifts. Tell her what you see. Tell him what you appreciate about him. Let each other know that they are loved deeply.

TAKE IT TO GOD

Before your date, spend some time in prayer with each other. Talk to God about some of the setbacks, pressures, and problems you're dealing with. Open up to Him about your concerns and fears. Ask Him to

- ▶ bless your time together on your Skyscraper Date;
- ▶ help you see things from His perspective—to recognize His ability to bring good things from bad situations;
- ▶ give you a sense of peace about the challenges you're facing—and a workable strategy for dealing with them.

DIG DEEP

The Bible makes it clear that the key to peace and fulfillment is being able to see things through God's eyes—to take an eternal view of our earthly circumstances. Here's where you'll find some of those passages.

- ▶ Proverbs 14:12
- ▶ Matthew 6:31–33
- ▶ 1 Corinthians 13:12
- ▶ Ephesians 3:18

- ▶ Philippians 4:6–7
- ▶ Devotional reading from *The Love Languages Devotional Bible*, page 1257

TO NEXT DATE

THE CAMPING DATE

WORDS TO GROW ON

*God created everything through him,
and nothing was created except through him.*

JOHN 1:3

*No human relationship can ever replace our
need for sharing life with God.*

GARY CHAPMAN

48

SET THE SCENE

The Camping Date allows married couples to
remove themselves from the "same old, same old"—
the routines and pressures of daily life—and literally
breathe fresh air into their relationship. This can be
accomplished in any number of settings, from the
most Spartan of campsites to the most luxurious
of cabins.

All that's really necessary is an opportunity to
commune with God and each other in a nature

setting—an opportunity to see, hear, smell, and experience things that are far from the everyday for you.

Whether you're spending a week in the heart of the Oregon wilderness or an evening in a makeshift tent in the backyard of your suburban home, a Camping Date may be just the change of pace you need.

MAKE IT HAPPEN

The Camping Date is one of the riskier propositions in this book. If it goes well, the results can be outstanding. If it goes badly, though, the results can be miserable. The problem is, there are too many variables beyond your control—weather and insects, to name a couple—that can negatively affect the outcome.

That's not to say you shouldn't give it a shot. You should. Just make sure you cover your bases first.

1 *You'll need to agree on a definition of "camping."*
One person's idea of "roughing it" may feel like luxury to someone else. In order to avoid unpleasant surprises later, you'll need to talk to your spouse about the kind of "camping" he feels most comfortable with. Does he lean toward the "Crocodile Dundee" end of the spectrum—content with just a rock for a pillow and a long knife for hunting? Or would she prefer a Holiday Inn within driving distance of a state park?

(Couples who aren't married may plan an evening-long campout in a backyard with a fire pit. Plan to roast marshmallows and make s'mores.)

2 Gather your supplies.
The nature and duration of your trip will determine the supplies you need. You can find starter lists at any number of online camping sites. Make sure you pack wisely, anticipating as many possible scenarios as you can think of.

If at all possible, test your equipment before you leave. Set up your tent in your yard and spray it with a hose to check for leaks. Make sure your flashlight batteries are good and your first-aid kit is fully stocked. The better you prepare for your trip, the better your chances are of avoiding unpleasant surprises.

3 Commune with God and each other.
Talk about the nature all around you—the beauty of God's creation. Celebrate it together. Let it draw you closer to Him.

FINISH STRONG

Before you end your Camping Date, spend a few minutes talking about the experience. Use the following questions as needed to guide your discussion.

- ▶ Agree or disagree? Spending time in nature is good for the soul. Explain.

- ▶ Agree or disagree? We spend enough time in nature. Explain.

- ▶ What does this setting tell us about God?

MIND YOUR LANGUAGE

If your date's primary love language is Quality Time, a campfire may be just what the doctor ordered. Plan to spend plenty of Quality Time in front of the fire, talking with your date or just enjoying the silence together. The longer you spend in front of the fire, the more love your sweetheart will feel.

TAKE IT TO GOD

Before your date, spend some time in prayer together. Praise God for the beauty of His creation. Share with Him some specific elements of creation that have made an impression on you. Ask Him to

▶ watch over you and keep you safe during your Camping Date;

▶ open your eyes to the elements of creation that often escape your attention in the busyness of daily life;

▶ help you learn to appreciate and acknowledge a different aspect of His creation every day.

DIG DEEP

Scripture is full of passages that offer praise and worship to God for the beauty of His creation. Here's a small sampling.

▶ Genesis 1:31

▶ Psalm 19:1

▶ Psalm 23:2–3

▶ Romans 1:20

▶ Colossians 1:16–17

▶ Devotional reading from *The Love Languages Devotional Bible,* page 1335

TO NEXT DATE

THE LEGO DATE

WORDS TO GROW ON

Anyone who listens to my teaching and follows it is wise, like a person who builds a house on solid rock. Though the rain comes in torrents and the floodwaters rise and the winds beat against that house, it won't collapse because it is built on bedrock.

MATTHEW 7:24–25

If you are married, nothing is more important than your marital relationship. It is the framework in which God wants you to invest your life and experience His love.

GARY CHAPMAN

49

SET THE SCENE

Can two adults really enjoy themselves with nothing more than a pile of small, brightly colored notched bricks? That's the question the Lego Date aims to answer. As with other dates in this book, the key is not necessarily the activity itself, but what it represents—and what it encourages you to talk about.

During your Lego Date, you will be building something as a team—just as you are in your life together. In order to be successful, you need to find a way to mesh your individual work habits, styles, and preferences. Ultimately, though, that meshing process may lead to a working relationship that is greater than the sum of its parts.

MAKE IT HAPPEN

Here's what you need to do in order to make your Lego Date a reality.

1 *Choose your medium.*
Don't let the name of the date limit you. You don't have to work with Legos. If your preferred medium is Lincoln Logs, by all means, use them. K'Nex pieces, wooden blocks, and dominoes are also acceptable substitutes. Decide whether you want to go freestyle (creating something of your own design) or build a model (following step-by-step instructions).

2 *Go the cheap route.*
If you don't own any Legos, look into borrowing some from your nieces or nephews, your neighbors, or your friends' kids.

3 *Aim for maximum togetherness.*
Whatever you build should be a joint venture, imagined and constructed by both of you. This isn't a time for delegating responsibilities (i.e., one person reading the directions and another doing the building). Both of you should be hands-on during the construction. The finished piece should represent you both equally.

4 *Use the building analogy as a jumping-off point for conversation.*

Make note of the fact that the two of you are building something together in your everyday life. You're building a relationship, a family, a life together, and a vehicle for God's work. Talk about how the "construction" has gone to this point. How well have you learned to work together? Are you satisfied with the results so far?

5 *Get some pictures.*

When you're finished, take a few photos of the two of you posing with your work. Call them mementos of your Lego Date. If you're especially proud of the finished product, post a few photos on your favorite social media site.

FINISH STRONG

Before you end your Lego Date, spend a few minutes talking about the experience. Use the following questions as needed to guide your discussion.

- ▶ What were some of the most challenging obstacles we faced when we started building a life together?

- ▶ What challenges do we face today?

- ▶ What do we want people to say about our relationship when the construction is finished?

MIND YOUR LANGUAGE

If your significant other's primary language is Receiving Gifts, buy a small Lego set, put it together, and give it as a reminder of the life you've built together.

TAKE IT TO GOD

Before your date, spend some time in prayer together. Thank God for your significant other—the coworker who's helped you craft a one-of-a-kind relationship. Thank Him for the influence that relationship has had on your life. Ask God to

- ▶ bless your time together during your Lego Date;

- ▶ help you maintain a spirit of cooperation and mutual respect for what the other person brings to the "building process";

- ▶ help you come away from your date with a renewed vision of what your relationship can be.

DIG DEEP

Though Legos are nowhere to be found in Scripture, you can find passages that fit the theme of building something together for your Lego Date. Here are some places to look.

- ▶ Deuteronomy 6:4–9
- ▶ Joshua 24:15
- ▶ Ephesians 5:1–2
- ▶ Ephesians 5:31–33
- ▶ Colossians 3:12–14
- ▶ Devotional reading from *The Love Languages Devotional Bible*, page 1280

TO NEXT DATE

THE FAMILY DATE

WORDS TO GROW ON

*Children are a gift from the Lord; they are
a reward from him. Children born to a young
man are like arrows in a warrior's hands.
How joyful is the man whose quiver is full of them!
He will not be put to shame when he
confronts his accusers at the city gates.*

PSALM 127:3–5

*Increasing numbers of young people
have not seen a demonstration of a
loving family and consequently
have little idea of where to begin.*

GARY CHAPMAN

50

SET THE SCENE

As a teenager, you likely thought of a date as a means
of getting *away* from your family—a chance to spend
quality time alone with your boyfriend or girlfriend.

Welcome to the wonderful world of adulthood, where a date can actually be *enhanced* by the presence of family members. At least, that's the theory behind the Family Date idea. By inviting carefully chosen relatives to join you for an evening of fun, you open the door to a world of possibilities.

You may hear stories about your significant other you've never heard before. You may discover where he gets certain traits or characteristics. You may get a deeper understanding of what makes her tick. At the very least, you may have a good time in the presence of people who are special to you both.

MAKE IT HAPPEN

The way you navigate the Family Date will depend on the personalities and family dynamics of the people you invite. If they're low-maintenance, you can plan a normal outing and have them accompany you.

If, however, they skew toward the high-maintenance end of the spectrum, you may need to adjust your planning. Perhaps your best strategy in that case is to invite the family for dinner and a movie . . . or dinner and an evening on the deck . . . or dinner and a walk around the neighborhood.

The plans themselves are secondary to the logistics. If you want to invite your date's mother, and you know her feelings will be hurt if you don't ask her to bring one of her world-famous apple pies, by all means, ask her to bring one of her world-famous apple pies.

Accommodate as many quirks as you need to (within reason) in order to create an atmosphere where fun, fellowship, and conversation can thrive.

FINISH STRONG

Before you end your Family Date, spend a few minutes talking as a couple about the experience. Use the following questions as needed to guide your discussion.

▶ What is God's will for your relationship with your family?

▶ What are some of the obstacles that get in the way of healthy, functional family relationships?

▶ What specific steps can you take to foster better relationships with your immediate and extended family?

MIND YOUR LANGUAGE

If your date's primary love language is Physical Touch, invite the huggingest, hand-holdingest, touchy-feeliest members of your family or your significant other's family to accompany you on your date. Encourage them to express their physical affection throughout your date. Working together, you should be able to fill your date's love tank by the end of the evening.

TAKE IT TO GOD

Before your date, spend some time in prayer together. If you've been blessed with a loving, caring, functional family, praise God for that. Thank Him for the fact that your family helped mold you into the person you are today. If, on the other hand, your immediate family *isn't* a source of love and affection for you, thank God for the other people in your life who have filled the void and shown you goodness and support. Ask God to

- ▶ bless your time with your date and other relatives during your Family Date;

- ▶ help you maintain a spirit of fun and camaraderie for the duration of your date;

- ▶ come away from your date with a renewed thankfulness and appreciation for the people with whom He's surrounded you—family members who care and want what's best for you.

DIG DEEP

The Bible is the original source of family values. Here are a few of the passages that emphasize the importance of family.

- ▶ Exodus 20:12
- ▶ Proverbs 1:8
- ▶ Proverbs 6:20
- ▶ Proverbs 22:6

- ▶ 1 Timothy 5:8
- ▶ Devotional reading from *The Love Languages Devotional Bible,* page 198

TO NEXT DATE

THE CAR DATE

51

WORDS TO GROW ON

*Above all, clothe yourselves with love,
which binds us all together
in perfect harmony.*

COLOSSIANS 3:14

*We cannot love others through our
own power, but we can love them
through the supernatural power
of the Spirit.*

GARY CHAPMAN

SET THE SCENE

Every date idea in this book is a celebration of love
—a way of enjoying God's gift of companionship.
Some of the ideas are frivolous; some are profound.
All are intended to bring you and your significant
other a little closer together.

The Car Date definitely falls in the frivolous category. This is not just a date idea; it's a challenge. Can you spend an entire evening with your sweetheart—in your car? Can you

- ► find a good place to eat;
- ► enjoy quality entertainment;
- ► keep the atmosphere lively and interesting;
- ► maintain a good conversation flow

. . . all within the confines of your automobile?

MAKE IT HAPPEN

You could probably kill a few hours in your car, and maybe have a few laughs along the way, without putting much thought into it. But if you really want to make an impression on your date— to give them a date they'll be telling their friends about—you'll need to do some planning.

1 *Brainstorm some creative, automobile-friendly forms of entertainment.*
Don't settle for, say, a fast-food joint with a drive-up window. Set your sights a little higher than that—perhaps a theme restaurant in your area with carhops or curbside service.

As for entertainment, you can't go wrong with a drive-in movie—as long as the movie is worth seeing. You could also drive through the campus of a local university—or take your car through a car wash. Use your creativity.

2 *Keep the conversation flowing (and thematic).*
In keeping with the auto-related theme of the date, swap some car stories with each other. Here are a few question prompts to spur your thinking.

- ▶ What's your earliest memory of riding in a car?
- ▶ What kind of cars did your family have when you were young?
- ▶ Where did you usually sit?
- ▶ How did you entertain yourself during car rides?
- ▶ What's the longest car trip your family ever took?
- ▶ What was your first car like?
- ▶ What happened the first time you ever got pulled over by a police officer?
- ▶ What's the closest call you ever had in a car?

3 *Know when to relax the rules for the date.*
If certain physical needs become urgent, feel free to temporarily suspend your no-leaving-the-car rule. Remember, your ultimate goal is to enjoy yourself—not to qualify for an official car-endurance record. In other words, don't get so hung up on the date's theme that you ruin the date's mood.

FINISH STRONG

Before you end your Car Date, spend a few minutes talking about the experience. Use the following questions as needed to guide your discussion.

- Agree or disagree? We have just the right amount of spontaneity in our relationship. Explain.

- Agree or disagree? This car could hold everything that's truly important to us. Explain.

- Agree or disagree? Our relationship brings glory to God. Explain.

MIND YOUR LANGUAGE

If your date's primary love language is Receiving Gifts, give a CD (on an actual disc or a digital download) of one of his or her favorite artists. Let him or her know that you spent some time trying to find just the right CD. Play it while you drive, and designate it the official soundtrack of your Car Date.

TAKE IT TO GOD

Before your date, spend some time in prayer together. Thank God for the fun and enjoyment in your life. Thank Him, too, for the gift of spontaneity—the freedom to shake things up by doing something out of the ordinary. Toward that end, ask God to

- bless your time together during your Car Date;

- help you maintain a spirit of fun and spontaneity throughout the evening;

- continue working in and through your relationship to bring glory to Him.

DIG DEEP

The Car Date involves two people in love enjoying life together. You can find several passages in God's Word that speak to those themes.

- Proverbs 17:22
- Proverbs 31:10–31
- Ecclesiastes 11:9
- 1 Corinthians 7:1–40
- Ephesians 5:25
- Devotional reading from *The Love Languages Devotional Bible*, page 1088

TO NEXT DATE

THE TV DATE

WORDS TO GROW ON

And now, dear brothers and sisters, one final thing. Fix your thoughts on what is true, and honorable, and right, and pure, and lovely, and admirable. Think about things that are excellent and worthy of praise.

PHILIPPIANS 4:8

We must concentrate on the present, which is in our hands to shape.

GARY CHAPMAN

SET THE SCENE

Couch potatoes need not apply. This date is designed for people who want to examine the messages—the obvious ones and the subtle ones—being conveyed by the media, for evidence of God's truth. In short, this date is designed for people who take seriously what they allow into their brains.

Think of this date as talking back to the screen—of pushing back against pushy broadcasters. The two of you will flip through the channels and react verbally to what you see—for better or worse. If you have a variety of programming options, you'll likely see shows you love, shows you used to like, shows you hate, and shows that make you question the future of civilization on this planet. The TV Date encourages you to talk about those reactions—and possibly reevaluate your media choices as a couple.

MAKE IT HAPPEN

Here are a couple of tips to consider for your TV Date.

1 *Make sure to have plenty of snacks or a fun meal planned.* Sure, TV dinners are an obvious choice. But if you can find some that are actually edible, why not take the obvious route? At the very least, you should be prepared with some popcorn—or, better yet, your date's favorite snack.

2 *Sample a variety of shows.* If you have time to prepare for your date, DVR a mix of programs: a reality show, a drama, a sitcom, a police procedural, some sci-fi, and maybe a few other things you've heard people talk about but haven't had a chance to watch yet. Watch a few minutes of each show—at least until you understand what's going on. Talk about the relative quality of it—the acting, the writing, the production values. Talk about the messages being conveyed. Are there any biblical principles to be found?

Talk about the artistic value. Does it offer any unusual perspectives or groundbreaking techniques?

Keep your observations casual and your conversation courteous. Agree to disagree when necessary.

FINISH STRONG

Before you end your TV Date, spend a few minutes talking with each other about the experience. Use the following questions as needed to guide your discussion.

- ▶ How well do we honor God with the amount of time we spend interacting with media?

- ▶ How well do we honor Him with the things we watch?

- ▶ What specific changes should we consider in our media-consuming habits?

 ## MIND YOUR LANGUAGE

When you're searching for shows to DVR, look for some of your significant other's favorite series. Record an episode (or more) and watch it at the end of your date. Your loved one likely will be

- ▶ flattered that you remember what her favorite show is;

- ▶ touched that you went to the trouble to record it;

- ▶ excited to watch it with you.

If her primary love language is Acts of Service, your gesture will have even more meaning for her. The fact that you went out of your way to find his favorite show will feel like love.

TAKE IT TO GOD

Before your date, spend some time in prayer together. Praise God for His gift of discernment —the fact that His wisdom is always available to us, through His Word and our conscience. Praise Him, too, for His gift of entertainment—the fact that people can use their talents and abilities to bring enjoyment to others. Ask God to

- ▶ bless your time together during your TV Date;
- ▶ give you the wisdom to evaluate and critique the things you watch in a way that honors Him;
- ▶ help you maintain that spirit of media discernment in your home long after your TV Date is over.

DIG DEEP

The Bible is big on discernment and making wise decisions— even those that involve our entertainment choices. Here are just a few of the passages that address those topics.

- ▶ Proverbs 3:1–35
- ▶ Proverbs 14:12
- ▶ Daniel 1:8
- ▶ Matthew 7:13–14
- ▶ Galatians 6:7–8
- ▶ Devotional reading from *The Love Languages Devotional Bible*, page 140

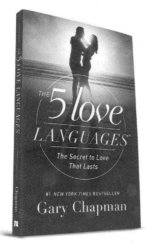